D0863094

PARISH FUNERALS

Michael Marchal

Liturgy Training Publications

Note on the first printing:

The *Order of Christian Funerals* was approved by the
bishops of the United States in November of 1985.
Though an implementation date of November 2, 1986
had been set, the OCF had not at that time received confirmation from the appropriate Roman congregation.
Parish Funerals is based on the text approved by the
bishops in 1985. Any alterations to that text will not be
reflected in these pages. Such alterations are expected to
be minor and will not affect the overall structure
envisioned by the OCF nor the order of the individual
rites.

Copyright © 1987, Archdiocese of Chicago. All rights reserved.
Liturgy Training Publications, 1800 North Hermitage Avenue,
Chicago IL 60622-1101; 312/486-7008.
Printed in the United States of America
ISBN 0-930467-65-5
Cover art by Suzi Novak
Design by Elizandro Carrington

CONTENTS

CHAPTER 1

THE ORDER OF CHRISTIAN FUNERALS

I was very lucky in college. My dorm had its own resident wise man. A Jesuit in his late fifties, he had been a missionary in India until health problems forced his return. Now he spent his time and energy on teaching theology, being dorm chaplain, and doing a great deal of counseling and retreat work. Though a bit vague in the classroom, he brought to spiritual direction an intensity which made him sought after and loved. We 60 undergraduates who lived in the dorm came to know him well. We saw his devotion at Mass and his keen bridge playing, his hour of prayer in the chapel and his love of a good drink. We saw his complicating health problems and his will to live and to work, his ups and downs, the good days and the bad. And we knew that he saw and understood ours as well.

Years after my graduation, an observation of his has remained with me. He would frequently comment: life is not a problem, it is a mystery. Passing courses, getting a date for the weekend, putting up with a cold—these were all problems. These we could dissect and analyze, we could come to grips with them. These were problems for us to deal with; we could take action.

But as Al used to say, the purpose of existence, the reality of love, the meaning of sickness and death—all those cosmic questions that bedevil us at 20—these we would never solve. They were mysteries, and we would have to live them. Insight would come, he assured us, but only at the price of experience. The only way we would ever know the reality of love was to live with someone for 30 years. We would discover the purpose of existence and the meaning of suffering by existing and suffering. And we knew we had before us in his own life the concrete example of his advice.

Al was articulating in his own words the biblical tradition. Our God is a living God, not the solution to life's problems. Only when we face our hopes, confusions, fears and pain with this "mysterious" outlook will we find insight and that "peace which passes understanding." "Sufferings bring patience . . . and patience brings perseverance, and perseverance brings hope." (Romans 5:3–4)

We can see this wisdom at work in the events surrounding death. Those who regard death as a problem try to solve it. Denial and camouflage are solutions. Those who treat death as a mystery are easy to spot. At the wake they are the ones who share the stories, tears and laughter. They are the ones who don't give trite explanations ("Her time had come") or banal comments ("He looks so alive"). Rather they are compassionate: they "suffer-along-with." They witness that our share in the mysteries of life is not private and isolated but communal. In the midst of loss and confusion and often rage, they are the ones who enable us all to say "*We* believe," when our personal faith would have trouble mustering "*I* believe."

Such is the heart and soul of those who would minister at the time of death. If we come to share in the hurt and confusion and mystery of death, then our faith in life will become apparent:

> The participation of the community in the funeral rite is a sign of the compassionate presence of Christ, who embraced little children, wept at the death of a friend, and endured the pain and separation of death in order to render it powerless over those he loves. (*Order of Christian Funerals*, #239)

The *Order of Christian Funerals* (OCF) challenges us on many levels. Like any liturgical book, it provides words to proclaim and rubrics for our rituals. It also provides something of the theological rationale and the human experiences that lie behind those words and rituals. Those who miss that will miss the heart of this revision of the 1969 *Ordo Exsequiarum*.

However, those who grasp the rationale and experiences that gird the OCF, and who make these rites their own, will receive a foundation for dealing with their own grief and with their ministry to others. It will be a disturbing book for them, filled with pain, tenderness and hope. They will ponder and pray over its introductions, find comfort and challenge in its texts, and discover at last ways to live it out with sincerity and grace. This commentary is offered in service to that work.

Any individual, bereavement group or liturgy committee that wishes to study the OCF should realize that their task involves their emotions, their faith and the rites of the church. They must realize that the task of adaptation is theirs. The OCF will become ours only as it gives shape and direction to the inner attitudes and the public worship and conduct of Catholics.

2

In no way is a commentary such as this to replace a thorough study and a firm familiarity with the text of the OCF. That text should be in the reader's hand for every page of this discussion. This book makes constant reference to the OCF, but it does not make a systematic effort to summarize it. That would not do it justice. This book is a companion, an introduction; it is not a substitute. Whether you have ever had occasion before to delve into a ritual book of the church or not, don't hesitate now. The OCF is a rich source of theology and reflection written for all, lay or ordained, who minister at the time of death. It will reach those who mourn and all the community only through your study and careful use.

Throughout this text, we offer the outlines of the various rites taken directly from the OCF. At the start, then, as a means of reference for your study, the table of contents of the OCF is given below. Use it to obtain an overview of the resources the OCF has to offer. Notice, for example, that the text of morning and evening prayer for the Office for the Dead is included as an integral part of the church's prayer. Notice also the kinds of texts made available in Part V: it is here that you will find many of the prayers and litanies newly composed for this book.

Order of Christian Funerals

Many of the rites identified in this list will be discussed in detail in this book.

Initial chapters of this guide to the OCF deal with general concerns: the broader sense of ministry envisioned by the OCF (chapter 2) and the various elements which are common to many of the rites (chapter 3). The following four chapters discuss the broad divisions of the funeral rites: the wake or vigil and other rites that precede the funeral liturgy (chapter 4), the funeral Mass or the funeral liturgy without Mass (chapter 5), the final commendation (chapter 6), and the rite of committal (chapter 7). Music for all of the rites is discussed further in chapter 8. The OCF offers an entire section on the funeral of a child; these rites and related matters are treated in chapter 9. A number of additional questions are discussed in the appendix.

Those who use this book, especially in a parish setting where it will be studied by various ministers or by a bereavement committee, will find it helpful to read through the entire text before attempting to discuss or plan for parish practice in any one area.

CHAPTER 2

LEADERSHIP IN THE ORDER OF CHRISTIAN FUNERALS

The vision of the church which received expression in the documents of Vatican II appears more and more in our official liturgical rites. The *General Instruction on the Roman Missal* (GIRM) echoes paragraph 28 of the *Constitution on the Sacred Liturgy* when it says:

All in the assembly gathered for Mass have an individual right and duty to contribute their participation in ways differing according to the diversity of their order and liturgical function. Thus in carrying out this function, all, whether ministers or laypersons, should do all and only those parts that belong to them, so that the very arrangement of the celebration itself makes the Church stand out as being formed in a structure of different orders and ministries. (GIRM #58. Cf. also #71–73)

The various reformed rites reflect this perspective. The document which had first guided the revision of Catholic funeral rites after Vatican II, the *Ordo Exsequiarum* of 1969, had also asserted a degree of communal responsibility in its section on "Offices and Ministries towards the Dead":

In the celebration of a funeral all the members of the people of God must remember that to each one a role and an office is entrusted. (*Ordo Exsequiarum* #16)

Yet the rest of the section and those following deal almost exclusively with guidelines for priests in preparing and planning the celebration of funerals. Deacons and laypersons are mentioned in #19 as substitutes when there is no priest available, but no description of any ministerial function apart from such substitution is given. The introduction of the new *Order of Christian Funerals* (OCF) is much more thorough.

In the section on "Ministry and Participation" the whole church as the ultimate minister is paramount. "Those who are baptized into Christ and nourished at the same table of the Lord are responsible for one another." (*Order of Christian Funerals*, #8) "The Church calls each member of Christ's Body—priest, deacon, layperson—to participate in the ministry of consolation." (#8) "The responsibility for the ministry of consolation rests with the believing community." (#9) Words of comfort and of faith, acts of kindness and of support in daily living, active participation in wakes and other funeral rites—all are suggested as ways of sharing in the total ministry. The dignity of all is resolutely affirmed.

Complementing that affirmation is an extended description of types of liturgical ministry performed by certain members within the community. The various tasks of readers, ushers, pallbearers, special ministers of the eucharist, may be carried out by laypersons, especially by those family members not overwhelmed by grief (#15). Organists or other instrumentalists, cantors, even a choir *should* assist the assembly's full participation (#33). Deacons, presented as ministers of the word, of the altar, and of charity (#14), should proclaim the gospel whenever there is a liturgy of the word (#24) as well as give the various admonitions to the assembly (e.g., #176). So important is respect for this diversity of roles that the OCF states (with unusual bluntness): "The presiding minister proclaims the readings only when there are no assisting ministers present." (#24)

The ministry of the priest is still given fullest description: "By giving instruction, pastors and associate pastors should lead the community to a deeper appreciation of its role in the ministry of consolation and to a fuller understanding of the significance of the death of a fellow Christian." (#9) The priest should provide advance information to families and should invite everyone to participate actively in funeral Masses, being sensitive to the feelings both of non-Catholics and of Catholics "who are not involved in the life of the Church" (#12).

The priest should help plan the funeral rites (#17) and give effective catechesis both on the "purpose and significance of the Church's liturgical rites for the dead" (#9) and on the psalms of the funeral rites (#25). Moreover, he should instill in lay ministers "an appreciation of how much the reverent exercise of their ministries contributes to the celebration of the funeral rites" (#15). The priest, as minister of reconciliation, should be especially sensitive to differences within families or to divisions between families and others. By being attentive, the priest can begin a process of reconciliation—a process that "may find expression in the celebration of the sacrament of penance, either before the funeral liturgy or at a later time" (#13). Finally, "priests as teachers of faith and ministers of comfort preside at the funeral rites, especially the Mass" (#14).

It is important to notice that, in this long list of obligations, the majority are not direct performance of a service but are rather ways of facilitating others in the performance of their ministries.

YOU CAN'T DO IT ALL

What will all this mean to Father Smith, pastor of St. Euphemia Parish? He has a major weekly homily to prepare, a school, a CCD program, and now a catechumenate that must be adequately staffed. He has an aging church building and a furnace that must be fueled and paid for. He has marriage paperwork and infant baptisms and confirmation coming up. And there are meetings night after night—parish council, school board, worship commission. He is not getting younger, and his last full-time assistant was just made a pastor—and will not be replaced because the 20-year vocation crisis just hit home. What can he do when a parishioner dies? Though he longs to be a source of comfort, every funeral Mass means he will be binating that day. He may be able to stop by the deceased's home during the day, but scheduled visitations at the funeral home are often in conflict with regular monthly meetings which he must attend.

More guilt and more energy will not solve Father Smith's problem. Accepting the vision of church proposed by Vatican II might. The OCF, built upon that vision, provides resources.

The current situation is clear in the directives. Priests "preside at the funeral rites, especially the Mass. . . . When no priest is available, deacons . . . preside at funeral rites. When no priest or deacon is available for the vigil and related rites or the rite of committal, a layperson presides" (#14). Moreover, "if pastoral need requires, the conference of bishops, with the permission of the Apostolic See, may decide that laypersons also preside at the funeral liturgy outside Mass" (#151). In other words, the entire sequence of funeral rites, except for what is particular to the funeral liturgy within the Mass, may now be conducted for a deceased Christian even when no ordained person is available. That final situation is not, and is nowhere in the OCF presented, as ideal, but it does present the average parish with an opportunity and a challenge to exercise the ministry of consolation in a new way.

Since Vatican II we have become accustomed to many forms of lay involvement in the parish. Perhaps the time is ripe to take seriously the expansion of bereavement ministry that has been occurring in many parishes. If Father Smith were to look around, he would probably find a pool of resourceful people. Homemakers whose children are now in school, retirees, self-employed or professional persons who set much of their own schedules—all are in some way available. Some of them might already have degrees or years of experience in nursing or psychology or social work or in another of the helping occupations. Some of them might be ordinary people who have lived life's joys and tragedies and can now share the faith that is in their hearts with others. Whatever the origin of their qualifications, Father Smith can call them forth, can see that they are appropriately trained, and then can empower them publicly as the church's representatives along with himself for the funeral rites. He will have done a truly priestly work.

MINISTER TO THE BEREAVED

Imagine what effect such an approach to team ministry would have at St. Euphemia's. Mr. Jones, an executive in his mid-40s, with a wife and three young children, dies late Monday night of a heart attack. Father Smith is notified but knows that he cannot see the family till Tuesday evening. Early Tuesday he phones Mrs. Grace, a woman in her 50s whose children are almost grown. She is a volunteer at the hospital and has been involved for a while in bereavement work.

Since Mrs. Grace is available to help, Father Smith telephones the deceased's family, tells them that he will be by that evening, and asks their permission for Mrs. Grace to work with them as the parish representative.

When Mrs. Grace learns they have approved, she telephones first for a convenient time and then visits in mid-morning. Her task is now twofold. First, she listens to their stories and their grief. Second, she plans out with them the funeral rites. Since the funeral director has already scheduled visitation for the next evening from 6 to 8 with a wake or vigil service at 8, and the funeral Mass for 9 the next morning, she has a great deal to do.

Mrs. Grace is very familiar with the scripture readings suggested in the OCF. She has decided beforehand which of these to suggest to the families for their consideration. She has selected perhaps a dozen readings in all, from which the families will choose two for the Vigil service and two or three for the Mass. Mrs. Grace can also explain the musical resources the parish has to offer. Since Mr. Jones was an amateur author, the family would like some of his poetry read during the services. She assures them that this may be done when a family member or friend speaks in remembrance of the deceased during the wake (#62).

Mrs. Grace also finds out if any of the family are competent and willing to serve as readers or communion ministers or if any friends could carry out those ministries. Lastly, in her own mind and in the discussion she is considering appropriate petitions for the general intercessions. Finally she leads the family in "Prayers after Death" from the OCF (#104–108).

Mrs. Grace has noticed how distraught the wife is over the suddenness of the death and how there seems to be some tension between her and her in-laws. She contacts Father Smith and alerts him to the situation. When he arrives at the family's home that evening, he knows that he will not need to do liturgy planning but rather must help the family deal with some of their differences during this time of grief. He too leads them in the "Prayers after Death," using the alternative prayer for a deceased husband (#398–35).

That afternoon, Deacon Brown, who has volunteered to lead the vigil, is told by Mrs. Grace what gospel text he will proclaim and preach on briefly the following evening. He also knows that the deceased's brother will speak on behalf of the family (and may include one of Mr. Jones' poems) just before the deacon gives the concluding blessing. A cousin who is a regular lector in the parish has also been alerted to what her reading will be. A cantor from the choir knows which music he will be expected to lead at the wake.

Father Smith now knows which readings will be the context of his homily at the Funeral Mass. The readers, communion ministers and acolytes have been designated. The parish music director knows what her responsibilities are.

On the morning of the funeral, Mrs. Grace joins the family at the funeral home before Mass and leads them in a brief service, "The Transfer of the Body to the Church" (#121–127), before the casket is closed and the cortege begins. At her invitation, the wife and children and the in-laws all join in the blessing before the casket is closed.

After the funeral Mass, Father Smith is free to go to the cemetery, so he will lead the rite of committal; otherwise, Deacon Brown or Mrs. Grace would have accompanied the cortege and led the committal. All the rites have two options for the concluding blessing; one is for use by a non-ordained person.

Such could be an ordinary funeral in a few years if we use the opportunity which the OCF provides us. Indeed, the scenario described does not even include some of the book's resources (e.g., "Gathering in the Presence of the Body"). Yet it does describe how clergy and laity can work together in a new and fruitful way within our common ministry of consolation.

WHEN THERE IS NO PRIEST

The story above presumes the availability of a priest—a presupposition which no longer can be made in a number of American dioceses and which will become more and more problematic as the number of active priests declines. The OCF has already faced that eventuality.

Except for the sacrament of penance and the celebration of eucharist, almost every responsibility listed for parish priests is stated as belonging as well to the other representatives of the church. The rubrics are written to direct the "minister" with the rank of that individual being specified only where a given task, such as proclaiming the gospel, is traditionally associated with a given order. In short, the OCF means that no Catholic needs to be buried without the visible presence and support of the church even if an ordained person is not available.

The one portion of the funeral rites where this point probably needs further exploration is in the rite given for the "Funeral Liturgy outside Mass." The liturgical, practical and pastoral reasons for celebrating the funeral liturgy are explored in #178. Real latitude is allowed in the place for the service. The parish church is preferred, but the service "may also be celebrated in the home of the deceased, a funeral home, parlor, chapel of rest, or cemetery chapel" (#179). The rites of final commendation and committal follow this funeral liturgy as they would follow the funeral liturgy with Mass.

Noteworthy is this statement about the funeral rite outside Mass: "The celebration may also include holy communion" (#180). The appropriate place in the service for communion is given in the rubrics (#195), and portions from the standard rite for communion from the reserved sacrament are reprinted at the end so that only one book is needed (#409—410). Included among the postcommunion prayers are several appropriate for funerals.

Such a situation, once again, is not presented as an ideal or as something to be encouraged. What was apparently important to the American bishops in approving these rites was the need of the people. As the OCF states in #154:

> Communion nourishes the community and expresses its unity. In communion, the participants have a foretaste of the heavenly banquet that awaits them and are reminded of Christ's own words: "Whoever eats my flesh and drinks my blood shall live forever." (John 6:55)

AN APPROACH TO MINISTRY

Certain observations should be made about the approach to ministry in OCF.

First, no specifications are laid down in the OCF for laypersons who are to function as the church's ministers. Neither age nor gender are mentioned. The only criteria are apparently competence and the minister's own worthiness to represent the church.

Second, if those who function as the church's ministers are to be competent, they need to be trained. Voice projection, body movement, knowledge of scriptural and liturgical options are as important as compassion and a spirit of prayer. Training in these areas demands some priority in the parish and the budget.

Third, and most crucially, a team approach to ministry can work only if the ordained publicly accept laypersons as genuine colleagues in the church's ministry. The ordained, especially priests, will determine the success or failure of the resources provided in the OCF. This will happen not only by their implementation of its liturgical changes but most of all by the way in which they adopt and carry out its vision of the church as community and of their role *within* that community. A sense of compassion and personal duty will drive some priests to try to do everything themselves. Not only will they "burn out," but new forms of ministry will be hindered.

Finally, there must be an acceptance of lay ministry by the laity. Talents and gifts must be respected and recognized, but a sort of neo-clericalism can easily creep in.

In short, we must *all* remain true to that vision of a "chosen race, a royal priesthood." With all of our flaws and hesitations and insensitivity we must work together towards becoming what our God constantly calls us to be, "the people set apart to proclaim the perfections of the One who has called us out of darkness into his own wonderful light" (1 Peter 2:9).

The OCF places all ministry within the context of the assembly of the baptized, the parish church. In #9 of the General Introduction, we find a direction that ought to inform the parish's every approach to burying the dead and consoling those who mourn:

> The responsibility for the ministry of consolation rests with the believing community, which heeds the words and example of the Lord Jesus: "Blessed are they who mourn; they shall be consoled" (Matthew 5:3). Each Christian shares in this ministry according to the various gifts and offices in the Church. As part of the pastoral ministry, pastors and associate pastors and other ministers should instruct the parish

community on the Christian meaning of death and on the purpose and significance of the Church's liturgical rites for the dead. Information on how the parish community assists families in preparing for funerals should also be provided.

In giving instruction, pastors and associate pastors should lead the community to a deeper appreciation of its role in the ministry of consolation and to a fuller understanding of the significance of the death of a fellow Christian. Often the community must respond to the anguish voiced by Martha, the sister of Lazarus: "Lord if you had been here, my brother would never have died," (John 11:21) and must console those who mourn, as Jesus himself consoled Martha: "Your brother will rise again. . . . I am the resurrection and the life: those who believe in me, though they should die, will come to life; and those who are alive and believe in me will never die" (John 11:25-26). The faith of the Christian community in the resurrection of the dead brings support and strength to those who suffer the loss of those whom they love.

CHAPTER 3

HOLY SIGNS

Since liturgical celebration involves the whole person, it requires attentiveness to all that affects the senses. (*Order of Christian Funerals*, #21)

Human creativity is a restless force within us, and every generation should have the chance to offer its talents in the service of God. We have a need and a right to take the symbols used in our rituals and make them our own.

A great obstacle to making our heritage of ritual and symbol truly ours is a pervasive minimalism. A few drops of water on the forehead is not the baptismal bath. A thumbprint of oil on the crown of the head is not an anointing. A poorly spoken prayer or a rushed reading of scripture is not worthy liturgical proclamation. Only ritual and symbol that physically mean what the words say they mean will evoke and express faith among the community.

A search for authenticity is particularly crucial with the symbols used in the funeral rites. The bereaved need the opportunity to express their deep feelings through symbols, and in their grief they are more open to the non-verbal message that those symbols can convey. Brief consideration will be given here first to various objects used in these rites, then to the scriptures and prayer texts. Those working with objects should be well versed in the U.S. bishops' document *Environment and Art in Catholic Worship.*

CANDLES

One of the major symbols in the funeral rites is the Easter candle.

The Easter candle reminds the faithful of Christ's undying presence among them, of his victory over sin and death, and of their share in that victory by virtue of their initiation. (#35)

To be authentic, this candle must be visible. We have all seen 18-inch Easter candles. Perhaps it has been reduced to that size so that a ten-year-old server can carry it. The entrance procession is then "led" by a symbol invisible to anyone not standing on the aisle.

The resolution of this problem lies not only in using an Easter candle of sufficient size but also in reconsidering children as servers. There are adults in almost every parish who are available even during the daytime and who would be willing and even flattered to take on such a ministry.

The essential element in the candle's decoration—indeed, what makes it an Easter candle—is the cross and the five wounds. The year's date and the Alpha and Omega proclaim that Christ's victory of the cross is real now and for eternity. The cross and the wounds proclaim the paschal mystery: Jesus who is now alive has passed through pain, crucifixion, and death itself. No other cross is needed, no other decoration for the candle is necessary if the markings on the candle are vivid and visible.

The former practice of placing other candles near or around the coffin during the funeral liturgy may be maintained if it is the local custom "as a sign of reverence and solemnity" (#35).

WATER

Another symbol used more than once in the ensemble of funeral rites is the sprinkling with holy water. This is primarily to "remind the assembly of the saving waters of baptism" (#36).

In the rites we inherited from the medieval church, holy water seemed to be used primarily for exorcism or absolution. Now it is a proclamation of the death and life into which the deceased entered through the waters of baptism. As a formula from the rite of Gathering in the Presence of the Body says:

> The Lord God lives in his holy temple yet abides in our midst. Since in baptism N. became God's temple and the Spirit of God lived in him/her, with reverence we bless his/her mortal body. (#114C)

Similar ideas are found in the reception rite and in the final commendation.

A few drops from what looks like a clothes-dampening bottle with a cross on it, or from a limed-up metal sprinkler, do not say "baptism." The hospital chapel, the funeral home, the parish and the cemetery should have on hand an attractive bowl or a pot to hold the water. If water is used at times when only a few people are present, no sprinkler is needed. Dipping one's hand in the water and sprinkling the body is a very simple, yet touching gesture. When a sprinkler is needed, it should be capable of dispersing water quite generously. Some parishes use branches from evergreen shrubs. Sometimes the family of the deceased will make a sprinkler out of a branch from their own shrubs and with flowers, all bound together with florists' tape.

INCENSE

During the funeral liturgy incense is used as a sign of reverence and of farewell during the final commendation and "as a sign of the community's prayers for the deceased rising to the throne of God" (#37).

What is needed is an attractive censer and incense which produces a pleasant aroma and abundant smoke. Not every commercial incense does this well. There is also a need to use the censer with dignity and style. A description of what is meant by "incensing crosswise" is found in the discussion of the final commendation (cf. p. 37).

THE PALL

The white pall is spread over the coffin during the reception rites at the church.

> A reminder of the baptismal garment of the deceased, the pall is a sign of the Christian dignity of the person. (#38)

The white pall is itself the symbol. There is no need to put more symbols upon it. A good, clean white cloth of an attractive weave that hangs well and has perhaps a border or an applique square at the corners speaks of being clothed in Christ's glory. There is no need for words or pictures sewed onto the cloth to distract from that message. If the design of this applique or border runs down the center of the pall, it is much easier to unfold the pall gracefully during the reception rites.

During these rites, the servers may carry the pall, but they are not the best people to place it over the casket. Some of the mourners (with the help of the funeral director) can do that. This gesture is another of those seemingly minor yet very moving ways in which the mourners can become part of the liturgical action.

Other Christian symbols may also be carried in the entrance procession and placed on or near the coffin, e.g., a Bible, a book of the gospels, a cross. Appropriate formulas for when these are used are found in OCF,

#400. Though individual circumstances might sometimes suggest using one of these symbols, in most cases the funeral liturgy does not need more symbols (cf. #21). We ought instead to do as best we can with those we already have.

The OCF includes a warning about which symbols may be used in the church itself:

> Only Christian symbols may rest on or be placed near the coffin during the funeral liturgy. Any other symbols, for example, national flags, or flags or insignia of associations, have no place in the funeral liturgy. (#38)

There is a place in the total ensemble of funeral rites for a ritual associated with military funerals or with various fraternal groups. But in the church's rites, the focus is on Christ's victory and our share in it. Another reason for such exclusion should be noted:

> The use of the white pall also signifies that all are equal in the eyes of God (see James 2:1–9). (#38)

One of the traditions of which Roman Catholics can be most proud is that everyone gets the same funeral liturgy.

VESTURE

The OCF has one short directive in terms of the color of vestments for the funeral rites: "The liturgical color chosen for funerals should express Christian hope but should not be offensive to human grief or sorrow." (#39) The 1969 rite's notes for use in the United States are repeated in the OCF: "White, violet or black vestments may be worn at the funeral rites." The current directive, which differs only slightly from the text found in #22 of the 1969 rite, should be read not only in terms of color, but of the whole mood conveyed by vesture and by other uses of fabric (the pall, altar covering, any banners). Sometimes these have offended against "human grief or sorrow" by their flippant use of slogans or decorations. As with all such matters, the choosing and making of vesture and other things used and seen in the funeral liturgy should be entrusted to those with a strong sense for the arts and for their place in liturgy.

THE LECTIONARY

In the selection of readings from the scriptures, OCF shows little originality. Nearly everything in OCF will be found in the present lectionary.

18

The previous list of seven Hebrew Bible (Old Testament) selections is unaltered. There are two new gospels, one being the death and burial of Jesus according to John (the narrative was already given from Mark and Luke). From the rest of the New Testament, the reading from the first portion of 1 Corinthians 15 is now given in a short as well as a long form and another selection from 2 Corinthians is provided. The total list for adult funerals still comprises only 45 selections—a rather small collection given both the beauty and diversity of the scriptures and the varied circumstances which surround death and burial.

The list may also be further shortened in practice because of the inaccessibility of some translations: readings that could speak to the situation are rejected by the mourners or the bereavement minister because of certain turns of phrase. What I mean can be most clearly seen in the divergent translations of the selection from Wisdom 4, especially verse 9. The New American Bible translation is:

Rather, understanding is the hoary crown for men, and an unsullied life, the attainment of old age.

The Jerusalem Bible has:

Understanding, this is man's grey hairs, untarnished life, this is ripe old age.

Though the Jerusalem Bible translation has its own inelegant language at times, it is an available option as is the Revised Standard Version. Most parishes probably own only one lectionary, and thus own only one of the three translations officially approved for the United States.

A diversity of translations, though, does not resolve the basic problem that bereavement ministers and clergy repeatedly express about the funeral lectionary: the restricted number of selections. There is, however, no rubrical requirement that only readings from the section "For the Dead" be used during the various funeral rites. The only requirement for the funeral liturgy itself deals with the *number* of readings:

Depending on pastoral circumstances, there may be either one or two readings before the gospel reading. (#138)

The subcommittee on funerals of the Cincinnati Archdiocesan Worship Commission has compiled the following list of suitable alternatives already found in the lectionary. The numbers given here refer to the location of the reading in every lectionary.

Proverbs 31:10–13, 19–20, 30–31 #158 A worthy wife is to be praised.
Ecclesiastes 3:1–11 #453 To everything there is a season.

Song of Songs 2:8–14 #198 Arise, my love, my dove, and come away!
Song of Songs 8:6–7 #731 Love is as strong as death.
Sirach 44:1,10–15 #606 I will praise our ancestors.
Isaiah 35:1–6,10 #7 Now will the eyes of the blind be opened.
Isaiah 41:8–10,13 #821–3 Fear not, I am with you.
Isaiah 57:15–19 #831–3 Peace! Peace to the far and near!
Isaiah 61:1–3 #719–6 God has sent me to comfort all who mourn.
Isaiah 65:17–21 #245 No longer will there be weeping or mourning.
Ezekiel 34:11–16 #173 I will watch over my sheep.
Ezekiel 37:12–14 #34 I will open your graves, my people.
Micah 6:6–8 #737–17 Do right, love goodness, walk humbly with God.
Zephaniah 3:16–20 #811–4 I will gather you up and bring you home.

Ephesians 3:14–21 #476 Experience a love beyond telling.
2 Timothy 4:6–8,17–18 #591 I have fought the fight and finished the race.
1 Peter 1:3–9 #44 We are given new birth into everlasting life.
Revelation 22:1–7 #508 We shall see God face to face.

Matthew 6:19–23 #369 Where your treasure is, there is your heart also.
Luke 1:67–74 #201 You shine on those who sit in the shadow of death.
John 3:13–17 #638 All who believe will have eternal life.
John 10:11–18 #915 I am the good shepherd.
John 10:27–30 #52 I give my sheep eternal life.

A bereavement minister needs acquaintance with the scripture texts. He or she then brings this knowledge to the service of the family, allowing them as much time as they wish to discuss possible readings. Such an occasion often has a deep effect on the members of the family.

PRAYERS OF INTERCESSION

The holy people of God, confident in their belief in the communion of saints, exercise their royal priesthood by joining together in this prayer for all who have died. (#29)

The intercessions are a form of petitionary prayer familiar to many Christians. They are *communal* in nature; this should always determine the form they take. Thus, the assembly's refrain and not the intentions are the primary aspect of the prayer. That is obvious in the traditional pattern for such intercessions: "For . . . ," or "That . . . , let us pray to the Lord." In this model the intentions are held before the community. Their response is the actual prayer: "Lord, have mercy" or "Lord, hear our prayer." Even those examples in the OCF which are modeled on other litany patterns still lead to a communal response.

In general, the intentions or petitions should be clear but brief. Most of the examples given in the OCF (see #401 and #407) are only one or two lines long. The petition should direct the community's prayer, not substitute for it.

If at all possible, the response should be sung. This can happen at funerals when it is the parish's normal pattern at Sunday Mass. Familiarity with this practice makes singing the intercessions possible even at the wake or the committal.

One of the assisting ministers, ideally the deacon or cantor, should proclaim the intentions. The OCF consistently gives such a rubric and suggests that family members, if able, should take on that liturgical role.

All involved in choosing texts for the intercessions should be familiar with the various examples found throughout the texts of the OCF and grouped together in Part V, #401 and #407. One pattern begins with a declarative statement and then moves into petition:

Many friends and members of our families have gone before us and await the kingdom. Grant them an everlasting home with your Son.
Lord, in your mercy!
R.   Hear our prayer.

Many people die by violence, war, and famine each day. Show your mercy to those who suffer so unjustly these sins against your love, and gather them to the eternal kingdom of peace.
Lord, in your mercy!
R.   Hear our prayer.   (#401-3)

Another pattern is similar to a litany with a very short invocation or title leading into the response. Some resemble one form of the penitential rite at Mass:

Risen Lord, pattern of our life forever!
Lord, have mercy.
R.   Lord, have mercy.

Promise and image of what we shall be!
Lord, have mercy.
R.   Lord, have mercy.   (#401-4)

Others are somewhat more elaborate:

You became a little child for our sake, sharing our human life.
To you we pray!

R.   Bless us and keep us, O Lord.

You grew in wisdom, age, and grace, and learned obedience
    through suffering.

To you we pray!

R.   Bless us and keep us, O Lord.   (#401-6)

Others are noteworthy not because of their structure but because of the
way their language is specific and descriptive:

For N., child of God and heir to the kingdom, that he/she be held
securely in God's loving embrace now and for all eternity.

We pray to the Lord.

R.   Lord, hear our prayer.

For N.'s friends, those who played with him/her and those who cared
for him/her, that they be consoled in their loss and strengthened in their
love for one another.

We pray to the Lord.

R.   Lord, hear our prayer.   (#401-7)

We have here adequate resources and some real inspiration for working
with this style of communal prayer. Our task is to adapt these to
circumstances and to learn to compose our own—a task which the OCF
sets before us (see #142).

THE PRESIDER'S PRAYERS

In the presidential prayers of the funeral rites the presiding minister
addresses God on behalf of the deceased and the mourners in the name
of the entire Church. (#28)

The Catholic tradition of prayer is richly diverse. Sometimes, as in the
intercessions, the entire assembled community is asked to voice aloud its
intercession for various needs. At other times, usually after such extended
vocal prayer by the community or after a period of communal silence and
reflection, the presider "collects" the prayers in a single prayer spoken in
the name of all.

From the variety of prayers provided the minister in consultation with
the family should carefully select texts that truly capture the unspoken
prayers and hopes of the assembly and also respond to the needs of the
mourners. (#28)

To help meet that rather awesome presidential responsibility, the OCF
has provided in Part V an expanded repertory of collects suitable for a
variety of circumstances: #397 is an index; #398 comprises 47 prayers for

the dead; #399 has 15 prayers for mourners. There are a variety of other prayers interspersed throughout the text.

Some of these prayers are noteworthy because they expand the traditional form of the collect. There are rhetorical questions:

Lord, in our grief we turn to you. Are you not the God of love who opens your ears to all? (#398-25)

And interjections:

How difficult to relinquish our charge; how difficult to trust in your ways! (#401-6)

There are some interesting images:

God of mercy,
look kindly on your servant N. who has set down the burden of his/her years. (#398-38)

And some that fail:

Confident that the petition of those who mourn pierces the clouds and finds an answer . . . (#398-40)

There are also new categories introduced to meet pastoral needs, e.g., a deceased non-Christian married to a Catholic, one who died accidentally or violently, one who died by suicide:

God of those who hope,
look upon our brother/sister N. tragically taken from our midst. Do not consider his/her sins nor judge him/her with the haste of a human heart. (#398-44)

With an ear for cadence and alliteration, this prayer truly can speak "from the heart" of the mourners who will hear it proclaimed.

The index is particularly useful. This rich collection of presidential prayers is meant for use not only as the opening prayer at the funeral liturgy but throughout the funeral rites. It demands, of course, that the presider become thoroughly familiar with these texts and that they be spoken with care and attention.

CHAPTER 4

THE VIGIL AND RELATED RITES

The Church through its funeral rites commends the dead to God's merciful love and pleads for the forgiveness of their sins. (*Order of Christian Funerals*, #6)

The celebration of the Christian funeral brings hope and consolation to the living. (#7)

Almost every adult has been through the experience: the phone call, the unexpected telegram, the relative who came to bring the news. Whether we have prepared ourselves or not, news of death always seems to have a sting to it. Someone's life has irrevocably ended—and ours must still go on.

Caught in such an inevitable transition, we search for support. Families, friends, the church—all have traditionally stepped in both to bury the dead with respect and to help the mourners through a difficult if not traumatic adjustment. As American Catholics, we should be proud of our rich heritage of concern and care and faith.

That rich tradition continues. Even as relatives scatter and neighborhoods fragment, the church is there. Indeed, in our mobile and often uprooted American society, the role of the church is possibly even more significant as other support has waned.

What do we as church have to provide someone who has just received the news of a death? Until 1969, we had a restricted perspective. Given the existing *Rituale Romanum*, we could provide the Requiem Mass. A beautiful and somber creation, the Requiem was dominated musically and thematically by the *Dies Irae* and climaxed in the rite of absolution. The forgiveness of the deceased's sins was the consistent, almost sole focus of the funeral. The *Rite of Funerals* of 1969 brought a broadening of that focus to include expression of our faith in the resurrection and consolation for the living. This quickly gained a welcome acceptance.

One by one, the revised rites of the 1960s are now being evaluated from the experience of more than a decade. *Pastoral Care of the Sick* was the first result of this process. Now, acting primarily through the International Committee on English in the Liturgy, the bishops accepted the new *Order of Christian Funerals*. With this new Order we have even more to offer those who come to us in their grief.

Contemporary American culture is death-denying. As a society we have come to presume that funeral directors should care for the "arrangements." We expect cosmetic embalming and inner-spring coffins. We have progressively separated ourselves from confronting the realities of dead bodies and their physical decay—in the name of sparing the bereaved. Yet such sincere sympathy can be misguided as it keeps mourners from concretely living through their grief.

The *Order of Christian Funerals* (OCF) in no way takes our eyes from the realities of physical death. Rather, it asks us to encounter those realities with the eyes of faith, to see in death a way in which we share Christ's paschal mystery. This *Order* is filled with the same spirit which enables us to sing on Good Friday, "By the wood of the cross you have brought joy to the whole world." Death is not denied here, but neither is the victory of Christ and the genuine peace which that victory brings to believers.

THE IMPORTANT PLURAL

We are asked to think of the funeral as many rites. For any funeral the OCF suggests a sequence of up to six times for ritual prayer. Adaptation of that sequence is expected: "The minister, in consultation with those concerned, chooses from . . . these . . . rites those that best correspond to the particular needs and customs of the mourners." (#50) It is clearly stated that "the Mass . . . is the principal celebration of the Christian funeral" (#5), but not the *only* celebration. What happens at the funeral home or wherever mourners gather by the deceased, what happens at the cemetery or the crematory, all is a matter of Christian concern and the church's ministry.

Perhaps the best way to capture the OCF's understanding of funeral rites (and that plural is basic to the understanding) is to envision a journey, or rather, two parallel journeys. The body of the deceased is moving from the place of death to the funeral home, to the church, and then to its final resting place. As the mourners accompany the body physically through all or part of that journey, they are—if the process is allowed to happen—moving inwardly as well. Intellectually, emotionally and spiritually they are step-by-step entering into a new relationship with the deceased, with themselves and one another. In pain and amid tears there is loss and separation, but "Christians celebrate the funeral rites to offer worship, praise, and thanksgiving to God for the gift of a life which has now been returned to God, the author of life and the hope of the just" (#5). The OCF offers a sequence of possible rites so that crucial moments of that outward and inward journey may be marked by appropriate prayer and the proclamation of faith. (Note that the first movement in this journey is already found in *Pastoral Care of the Sick*, chapters 6 and 7: "Commendation of the Dying" and "Prayers for the Dead." These are rites to be kept at the time and place of death.)

THE RITES WITH THE FAMILY

Although the vigil or wake is intended to be the principal rite in the time between death and the funeral liturgy (#54), three other rites are provided. The first is simply named "Prayers after Death"; it "provides a model of prayer that may be used when the minister first meets with the family following death" (#101).

Outline of the Rite: Prayers after Death

Invitation to Prayer
Reading
The Lord's Prayer
Concluding Prayers
Blessing

Consisting primarily of a few verses from scripture and the Lord's Prayer, the rite is intended for use either immediately after death or as the principal part of a first pastoral visit. The rite normally will depend on the presence of the church's representative and his or her familiarity with the prayers which "can comfort the mourners as they begin to face their loss" (#102).

Among the prayers is that series of responses familiar to us before the 1969 revision: "Eternal rest grant unto him/her, O Lord." To accompany these familiar words, some appropriate gesture is suggested. The proposed gesture is making the sign of the cross upon the forehead of the deceased, but some other gesture may be employed. The experience of some in bereavement work is that an invitation to come into physical contact with the deceased is psychologically and pastorally sound. Marking the body with the sign of the cross can be both comforting and the beginning of the inward process of letting go. Especially if everyone present could share in the gesture by laying their hands on the body, a sense of common support would be created.

The second rite provided is a model for prayer to be used by the family, "Gathering in the Presence of the Body." This may take place either before or after the body's preparation for burial.

Outline of the Rite:
Gathering in the Presence of the Body

Sign of the Cross
Scripture Verse
Sprinkling with Holy Water
Psalm
The Lord's Prayer
Concluding Prayer
Blessing

This moment is crucial. "The family members, in assembling in the presence of the body, confront in the most immediate way the fact of their loss and the mystery of death." (#109) The rite's emphasis again is upon presence and familiarity. The church "seeks to be with the mourners in their need and to provide an atmosphere of sensitive concern and confident faith" (#110). The OCF provides brief selections from scripture and the Lord's Prayer. This rite could be of real benefit for mourners at a preliminary viewing of the body arranged for the immediate family before a general visitation, or could possibly be combined with or substituted for the vigil in certain circumstances. Many parish priests find it increasingly difficult to be present for the evening vigil or wake service. Instead, they have found that their presence at this first viewing of the body, usually in the afternoon, is not as difficult. Even more, this intimate time is much better suited to the priest's ministry to the immediate family. The flexible and simple rite provided in the OCF brings a proper tone and beauty to these moments.

With pastoral soundness, this rite provides two gestures. The traditional sprinkling with holy water is suggested, accompanied by three optional formulas that are not exorcisms or absolutions but reaffirmations of baptism. It may be that asking others present to share in the gesture, possibly by repeating it individually, would have some pastoral merit.

The second gesture provided is a repetition of that marking with the sign of the cross described above. Even if this is being done a second time, it can be a strong moment for the family. One problem might arise, though, from the common North American style of preparing the body: smearing the cosmetics applied to the face would be unpleasant for all concerned. Consultation with the funeral director beforehand would avoid any difficulties here. Funeral directors will want to encourage these pastoral practices and their advice may be of great help. An alternative gesture such as the sign of the cross over the body, then laying a hand upon the deceased's shoulder, might be effective.

The third rite, "Transfer of the Body to the Church or to the Place of Committal," would probably occur most frequently after the wake, though in many cases parishes now allow the use of the church for wakes. Some religious communities use their chapels in a similar fashion. In this case, the rite of transfer would precede the wake. The rite is suitably led by a member of the family or by the funeral director.

Outline of the Rite: Transfer of the Body

Invitation
Scripture Verse
Litany
The Lord's Prayer
Concluding Prayer
Invitation to the Procession
Procession to the Church or to the Place of Committal

The transfer of the body can be a moment of great emotion. The journey of separation is beginning (#120), and the mourners need the support of faith to undertake it. This is found in the invitation to the procession. After a brief reading from scripture, a litany, and the Lord's Prayer, the church's representative speaks to those present:

The Lord guards our coming in and our going out. May God be with us today as we make this last journey with our brother/ sister. (#126)

There is nothing in this rite to accompany the closing of the casket. This seems to me an unfortunate omission. A simple marking with the sign of the cross while praying "Eternal rest . . ." could be appropriate and effective. Repetition of what has become familiar is strengthening at such moments.

Turning to what the OCF regards as the principal service aside from the funeral itself, the "vigil" or wake, we find a format that allows for great variety.

Outline of the Rite: Vigil for the Deceased

Introductory Rites

Greeting
Opening Song
Invitation to Prayer
Opening Prayer

Liturgy of the Word

First Reading
Responsorial Psalm
Gospel
Homily

Prayer of Intercession

Litany
The Lord's Prayer
Concluding Prayer

Concluding Rite

Blessing

Alternative Outline:
Vigil for the Deceased with Reception at the Church

Introductory Rites

Greeting
Sprinkling with Holy Water
[Placing of the Pall]
Entrance Procession
[Placing of Christian Symbols]
Invitation to Prayer
Opening Prayer

Two versions of the introductory rites are provided. The first is for use in a person's home or a funeral home or a chapel or any suitable place. The second, for use when the wake is in the church, begins with the rites usually associated with the reception of the body at the funeral liturgy itself, then continues as in the first version.

Also provided are both morning and evening prayer for the dead from the liturgy of the hours with a selection of alternative hymnody. These may be preceded by the "Reception of the Body" and may lead into the procession to the place for the rite of committal. Such an ordering would occur especially at morning prayer when the funeral liturgy has been celebrated the previous evening (#348). Though this celebration of morning and evening prayer will probably not be the more frequently used format, those parishes and religious communities familiar with this form of communal prayer will welcome its integration into the sequence of funeral rites.

Whatever structure is chosen for the wake, two points stand out very clearly in the OCF, and each raises questions and poses challenges. First is the communal nature of the service: "At the vigil the Christian community keeps watch with the family in prayer to the God of mercy." (#56) If our local or family customs presume that the wake is merely a time for individual visitation with the deceased and the mourners, the new *Order* asks us to broaden our vision. This is in no way intended to discourage such individual visitation, but to encourage complementing the practice with some form of communal rite. Ordinary experience tells us how much this service is needed, especially when the timing of the funeral Mass makes it impossible for many to attend. However, the vigil service cannot achieve its purpose if it is merely a "time-out" during the coming and going of the visitation. Over the years, parishes and funeral directors can build up an expectation that the vigil service is to take place at a certain time and that it is a true high point in the support and prayer which parishioners bring to the family. Leadership will probably come to reside with deacons and members of the bereavement committee.

The second point is that, whatever the format, the purpose of the vigil is to proclaim the word of God: "The proclamation of the word of God is the high point and central focus of the vigil." (#59) "In this time of loss the family and community turn to God's word as the source of faith and hope, as light and life in the face of darkness and death." (#56) This emphasis asks us again to reexamine what we consider customary—not to abolish what is familiar and beneficial but to keep all our prayers in touch with the root of our faith as we hear and respond to the word of God.

Both pastoral sensitivity and artistry are needed in preparing the vigil. The OCF insists repeatedly that adaptations must be made to time, place, number of participants, available resources, faith of the deceased and of the mourners, ethnic traditions, and so on. We are thus called to take seriously the task of integrating the wealth of our popular heritage with official liturgy in a way that we have seldom done.

OBSERVATIONS AND OPTIONS

The vigil as given is devoid of gesture, other than the possible marking of the forehead of the deceased with the sign of the cross which was discussed above. Moreover, both here and in the funeral liturgy the rubrics insist that the homily is to be based upon the word of God and is not to be a eulogy (#61 and #141). However, the opportunity is given between the concluding prayer and the blessing for a member or friend of the family to speak in remembrance of the deceased (#96). And in the directions for the vigil of a deceased child, it is suggested that "other elements or symbols that have special meaning for those taking part may be incorporated into the celebration"(#246).

Including such reminiscences in the wake has been both moving and fitting to the occasion. Sometimes this is a more formal talk, but more often it is informally shared memories of the deceased. Scrapbooks, mementos, and sometimes children's art, either just scattered about or reflected on aloud, can be quite fitting. Concrete, personal reminiscence within the context of faith and amid the more intimate setting of a funeral home or a chapel works marvels of healing and consolation among the grieving. All of this is especially important if, as is most often the case, the wake is an assembly of persons who knew the deceased in quite different ways. Such sharing will always bring to each a more complete knowledge of the person who has died. Family members who have lived at a distance will appreciate stories of a brother or sister whose life they now need to complete.

The wake, rather than the funeral Mass, is the time for such intimate sharing. Mementos which are out of place at Mass work well in a more intimate setting where they can be handled, passed around, mulled over—not just put on display.

CHAPTER 5

THE FUNERAL LITURGY:
THE MASS

In this chapter we will discuss chapters 3 and 4 of the *Order of Christian Funerals:* "Funeral Mass," and "Funeral Liturgy outside Mass." However, the rites of commendation which are part of this funeral liturgy will be treated in our next chapter.

Outline of the Rite:
Introductory Rites of the Funeral Mass

Greeting
Sprinkling with Holy Water
[Placing of the Pall]
Entrance Procession
[Placing of Christian Symbols]
Opening Prayer

According to Vatican II the primary actor in any Roman Catholic liturgy is the congregation, the assembly. The ministers (ordained or not), including the musicians, are present not to perform *for* the community but rather to direct the community in action and to prompt them in prayer. This fact is crucial in these introductory rites.

First, where is the congregation? If the majority are arriving with the cortege, then one approach to these rites would be taken. If most people will already be gathered in the church, other possibilities open up. The weather and physical layout of the building are also important.

The ideal is for the reception rite to be celebrated at the entry of the church.

The church is at once a symbol of the community and of the heavenly liturgy that the celebration of the liturgy anticipates. (*Order of Christian Funerals*, #131)

The building called church must serve the community which is the church. How can this happen?

If most of the participants in the funeral Mass are arriving in the cortege and the weather is good and the space available, then it is best to have everyone gather in front of the church or in the entryway for the reception rite, then escort together the body of the deceased into the place of assembly.

If most of the participants arrive before the cortege, or if the weather is unfavorable, then it is best to celebrate the rites at the entrance to the nave. Everyone already present turns to face the casket and family. This would still create a sense of welcome to the assembly and its gathering place. When the room is not full, the reception rite is best celebrated in the middle of the church. Those seated in front turn around, and the mourners fill the aisle behind the coffin. It should always be physically obvious that the gathered people, and not the presider alone, do the receiving, the welcoming.

Moving the coffin into place and seating the family before the service begins destroys the purpose of the reception rites: to mark a crucial stage of a journey. The *focus* is to be the community's welcoming of the deceased and the mourners; the words and gestures of the presider over the coffin only give expression to this.

Gathering everyone at the entryway has another good effect: after processing together to the front, people will sit around the family in the front rows. When this type of welcoming for the body and family is not done, some attention should be given to a parish practice which encourages all present to fill the front of the church. Too often the family is isolated: rows of empty pews around them. This hardly speaks of the faith our liturgy celebrates. Perhaps the ministry of usher, some of which is taken over by funeral directors, needs to be emphasized at every parish funeral. Part of the ushers' work would be to leave only enough front pews for the family (determined by consulting the family beforehand), then to seat everyone else as far forward as possible.

Music is part of the rite of reception:

To draw the community together in prayer at the beginning of the funeral liturgy, the procession should be accompanied, whenever possible, by the singing of the entrance song. (#135)

Attempting to sing from a text while a major portion of the congregation is moving does not draw the community into prayer. One possibility is an extended prelude which allows most people to reach their places before the song begins. A better solution is to select a song with a familiar refrain. The OCF suggests this (#135) when it proposes using one of the alternative songs of farewell (#403) as a processional song. Whatever choice is made, the sensitivity of the musicians to the many circumstances of weather, size and age of the congregation is absolutely crucial.

An important detail about the reception rite is courtesy. The ministers must *never* keep the mourners waiting. The ministers are to be waiting at the entrance when the cortege arrives. This shows respect for the emotional condition (and often the age) of the mourners; it indicates the proper ministerial role of the presider, and helps create the hospitality of the church. There needs to be time then for the coffin to be put in place, for the mourners to line up, and for informal greetings to be exchanged between the ministers and the mourners. Holy water and the pall, both used in the reception rites, were discussed in chapter 3.

When the reception rites at the church precede the wake, rather than the Mass, these same considerations about weather and size of the congregation still apply. If the wake is held in a side chapel or adjoining room, it may be best to postpone the reception rite until the funeral liturgy itself. On occasions when the Mass is to begin without the reception rite, careful prior consideration should be given to which form of the penitential rite would be most suitable; C-6 or C-7 from the sacramentary would usually be appropriate. Note that apart from this, the sacramentary is not needed until the prayer over the gifts since all other texts are found in the OCF.

The opening prayer concludes these introductory rites. Prior consideration and preparation of the most appropriate text from #164 or #398 is essential.

THE LITURGY OF THE WORD

This portion of the service proceeds as usual. If there are two readings before the gospel, it is preferable as always to have a different reader for each (#138). The responsorial psalm and the gospel acclamation should be sung if at all possible (#139 and #140). A homily should always be given but it should not be a eulogy (#141). Someone may speak in memory of the deceased at the wake or before the final commendation (#96 and #170). The liturgy of the word concludes with the general intercessions (#142, #167, #193 and #401), an important portion of the liturgy if done well.

The readings found in the lectionary were discussed in chapter 3. For a general study of the liturgy of the word and the liturgy of the eucharist, see *The Liturgy Documents* and *Liturgy with Style and Grace* (Liturgy Training Publications). The care a parish regularly gives to its Sunday liturgy will be manifest here.

THE LITURGY OF THE EUCHARIST

It is appropriate that candles, the altarcloth, and a small arrangement of flowers be brought forward along with the bread and wine during the preparation of the altar and the gifts. A simple procession is an effective way of involving people here. Again, regular Sunday practice would usually determine the practice at the funeral Mass.

Incense may be used here. The OCF suggests that the body be incensed only once (#173). The final commendations seems the more appropriate time. If incense is used during the preparation of the gifts, it might be best to use it only to honor the gifts themselves, the altar, and perhaps the assembly.

Eucharistic Prayer III with its extended memento of the dead is a popular and appropriate choice. However, it is not the only option. There are eight other approved eucharistic prayers and at times one of these could be especially fitting. The two prayers for reconciliation are especially noteworthy. The acclamations for the eucharistic prayer are among the core musical elements of the service (#144).

The possibility of distributing communion under both species, if not already the norm, should be given serious consideration. After communion, a time of silence and stillness is important. This leads to the prayer after communion. When the liturgy of the eucharist is thus concluded in a quiet simplicity, the assembly and ministers are prepared for the final commendation.

THE FUNERAL LITURGY OUTSIDE MASS

This form of the funeral liturgy may be chosen rather than the Mass for several reasons:

- when the funeral Mass is not permitted, namely, on solemnities of obligation, on Holy Thursday and the Easter Triduum, and on the Sundays of Advent, Lent, and the Easter Season
- when in some places or circumstances it is not possible to celebrate the funeral Mass before the committal, for example, if a priest is not available
- when for pastoral reasons the pastor and the family judge that the funeral liturgy outside Mass is a more suitable form of celebration (#178)

A priest is the ordinary presiding minister at this service; in the absence of a priest, a deacon is the ordinary presider. If pastoral need requires, the OCF notes that a layperson may preside (#151 and #182). The other ministers— readers, acolytes, musicians—are needed and function as they normally would.

This liturgy begins with the reception of the body and includes the full liturgy of the word. The Lord's Prayer concludes the general intercessions and leads to the final commendation.

Outline of the Rite:
Funeral Liturgy outside Mass

Introductory Rites

> Greeting
> Sprinkling with Holy Water
> [Placing of the Pall]
> Entrance Procession
> [Placing of Christian Symbols]
> Invitation to Prayer
> Opening Prayer

Liturgy of the Word

> Readings
> Homily
> General Intercessions
> The Lord's Prayer

If the reception rite has already been done as part of the wake, the liturgy begins with an entrance song, a greeting, an invitation to prayer, and the opening collect—but without the penitential rite (#136 and #183).

The OCF seems to presume that holy communion will not ordinarily be part of this liturgy. However, #195 does indicate that holy communion can be distributed and refers the minister to Part V, #409 and #410. These are taken from *Holy Communion outside Mass* and are included in the OCF as an appendix. There is no reference to when the sacrament is brought from the place of reservation to the table. Presumably, this would be done before the Lord's Prayer as is normally the practice in distributing communion outside Mass. This avoids undue haste and the unfortunate practice of distributing communion directly from the tabernacle. Bringing the sacrament to the table with reverence, genuflecting, then inviting the Lord's Prayer, allows this prayer to be the preparation for holy communion.

The normal practice in the rite for distributing communion outside Mass would also allow the minister to invite those present to share the peace greeting after the Lord's Prayer. Though this has not been mentioned in #409, it would be quite consistent with the inclusion of holy communion in this liturgy.

When communion is then distributed, a time of silence should follow leading to the prayer after communion (several options are provided in #410). After this, the minister approaches the coffin for the final commendation.

EVENING FUNERAL MASSES

Certainly, in times past, it was easier for the parish to gather during the day. In our own time, employees ordinarily leave work to go to a funeral only if the deceased is a member of the immediate family. The problem is that our funeral Masses held on weekday mornings are more often than not exclusively family affairs, lacking the important presence of a wider parish community. It is ironic that while many people will come to an evening vigil, the next morning finds precious few assembled to celebrate the eucharist.

The solution is not going to come from places of employment. The solution is to schedule the funeral Mass at a time when members of our parishes can assemble around one of their own. This would suggest that weekday evenings would be given a high priority in the scheduling of the funeral eucharist.

Evening funeral Masses, usually followed by burial next morning, are discouraged by many funeral directors for the same reasons they are resisted by many parishioners; people assume such evening funerals are somehow inconvenient (they may necessitate a trip with the body from the church to the mortuary) or exceptional. A parish policy encouraging the scheduling of funerals at evening, and the experience of these liturgies as normal, would help them become parish affairs once again.

CHAPTER 6

THE FUNERAL LITURGY: THE FINAL COMMENDATION

Do not go gentle into that good night. . . .
Rage, rage against the dying of the light.
—*Dylan Thomas*

Thus did the Welsh poet put into words his feelings about the death of his father— in a work that appeared only a year before his own death at age 39. In these few words he has caught the loss that accompanies the death of someone close to us. Even when death brings a welcome end to the infirmities of age or the agony of disease, something precious has been taken from us. In the face of such loss come disappointment and regret and even anger that rises within us.

Yet regret and anger are not the last words of grief. Even when the loss is most bitter, we believe that hope and love and the power of the risen Jesus are present. All of this is present in the strongest moment of these rites that take us from the deathbed to the grave. That is the "Final Commendation" which concludes the funeral liturgy (whether this is the "Funeral Mass" or the "Funeral Liturgy outside Mass"). We speak here of those final moments before the body is taken from the church.

Sadly, this moment of final commendation has seldom had in parish practice the full impact that it should have within the total sequence of funeral rites.

A PORTA INFERI

The "Final Commendation and Farewell" was the last element of the total ensemble of Western Christian funeral rites to develop (cf. Richard

Rutherford, *The Death of a Christian: The Rite of Funerals*, New York: Pueblo, 1980, pp. 56-65). The funeral journey from the home of the deceased to the place of burial had traditionally included a "station" at the church. This stopover grew longer during the eighth and ninth centuries as it came to include the celebration of the eucharist. Consequently, a transition into the final phase of the interrupted journey was needed.

At first, texts for this rite were lifted from the bedside service of commendation following a death. But soon this commendation at the church came to reflect the Middle Ages which created it. It was dominated by a sense of individual sinfulness and pessimism in the face of the last judgment—those attitudes which most vividly separate the medieval outlook on death from that of the earliest centuries of Christianity. For the *Subvenite* ("Saints of God") responsory there was substituted the *Libera me* ("Deliver me") with its dark images of human wretchedness on the day of wrath. Indeed this very responsory was ultimately versified as the famous sequence *Dies Irae*. Finally, in the 12th century, holy water and incense were added to the rite as familiar gestures for solemn exorcisms and blessings. Thus the rite which the medieval church fittingly named "The Absolution" was complete. (It is an interesting bit of history that a rite of *five*—count them—absolutions evolved for bishops and civil dignitaries. The happy life of the simple faithful!)

The order of funerals, *Ordo Exsequiarum*, which we began to use in 1969, officially changed the medieval emphasis on absolution by going back to the rite's original significance.

> The meaning of the rite does not signify a kind of purification of the deceased. . . . Rather it stands as a farewell by which the Christian community together pays respect to one of its members before the body is removed or buried. (*Ordo Exsequiarum*, #10)

The "Saints of God" responsory was restored in place of the "Deliver me," and the concluding prayer spoke now of thanksgiving and commendation rather than of diabolic attacks and the pains of hell.

The 1969 service was most forceful about music in this rite. The "Saints of God" responsory was given in the official text, but any suitable song could be substituted—as long as it could be sung by *all* those gathered.

> Not only is it useful for all to sing this song, composed of a pertinent text set to a suitable melody, but all should have the sense of its being the high point of the entire rite. (*Ordo Exsequiarum*, #10)

Gesture was also kept in the rite, but the medieval sense of exorcism was reinterpreted.

Also to be seen as signs of farewell are the sprinkling with holy water, a reminder that through baptism the person was marked for eternal life, and the incensation, signifying respect for the body as the temple of the Holy Spirit. (*Ordo Exsequiarum*, #10)

The purpose of this revised rite was to help the mourners experience a turning point in their grieving. In silent prayer and song, with gesture and ministerial prayer, the Christian community was to bid farewell in Christ to one of its members—until the day of resurrection.

We have generally failed to capture this vision of the restored Final Commendation and Farewell. We might as well be performing the medieval absolution service. Seldom is there singing at this point in an ordinary parish funeral. Neither the "Saints of God" nor alternative responsories have caught on. Nor has any other "pertinent text set to a suitable melody" become part of our common repertory.

Gesture has also disappeared from the rite. Since gestures were not to be duplicated, the sprinkling with holy water as a reminder of baptism has become in the United States firmly identified with the reception of the body at the church. Incensation has generally become identified with the presentation of the gifts.

The texts—which were to be recited when singing was impossible—did not help create a new vision for us. The first option, "Peace be with those . . ." required a clumsy alternation between two ministers and the congregation and was thus too difficult to manage. In most instances we seem to have fallen back on the second option, the (usually tedious) recitation of the "Lord, save your people" litany, which sounds much more like an exorcism than a Christian farewell. Here more than anywhere else we need both to reassess our performance of this rite and to envision its possibilities.

USING THE REVISED RITE

The new *Order* shares the same vision of this rite as the 1969 *Ordo Exsequiarum*.

The final commendation is a final farewell by the members of the community, an act of respect for one of their members, whom they entrust to the tender and merciful embrace of God. (*Order of Christian Funerals*, #146)

The structure remains identical to the 1969 rite, as do most of the basic prayers, though in new translations. The rite's outline is simple:

Outline of the Rite: Final Commendation

Invitation to Prayer
Silence
[Sign(s) of Farewell]
Song of Farewell
Prayer of Commendation
Procession to the Place of Committal

The ministerial invitation to prayer with which we have been familiar (which sounded more like a litany than an invitation with its succession of "May . . ." clauses) has been placed in the "Additional Texts" section at #402. Two shorter and much more direct invitations have been moved from the appendix to primary place in the body of the text. Out of the total number of five invitations, these two are probably the most straightforward calls to recollection and faith and farewell. The first reads:

> Before we go our separate ways, let us take leave of our brother/sister. May our farewell express our affection for him/her; may it ease our sadness and strengthen our hope. One day we shall joyfully greet him/her again when the love of Christ, which conquers all things, destroys even death itself.

Yet the minister is free to speak in his/her own "similar words." Especially since none of these five invitations is adapted to the diverse situations that we so often meet (e.g., one who died violently, a young parent), a composition that speaks to the moment can be powerful. Without turning into a eulogy, this invitation can help us to enter more deeply into the process of saying farewell. Option 2 in #402 can easily serve as the basis for such an adaptation:

> Our brother/sister N. has fallen asleep in Christ. Confident in our hope of eternal life, let us commend him/her to the loving mercy of our Father and let our prayers go with him/her. He/she was adopted as God's son/ daughter in baptism and was nourished at the table of the Lord; may he/ she now inherit the promise of eternal life and take his/her place at the table of God's children in heaven.
>
> Let us pray also on our own behalf, that we who now mourn and are saddened may one day go forth with our brother/sister to meet the Lord of life when he appears in glory.

Whatever is said should be prepared beforehand. An essential element in such invitations is brevity. Whatever words are chosen, the minister must always remember that he/she is *not praying* here but *calling others* to prayer, not addressing God but rather the community.

That same ministerial restraint is essential for the second element in the rite—silence. If the call to prayer is longer than the silence, there is an imbalance. Both the minister and the songleader should respect the prayer that is going on in the minds and hearts of the assembly.

The third element, the signs or gestures of farewell, raises certain questions. Sprinkling with holy water is part of the reception rite; its repetition here is ordinarily unwise. Yet the rite needs actions and not just words. Incensation can work if done with more energy and style. Rather than our usual Western funeral style of swinging a little smoke over the top of the coffin during a quick once around, the gesture could be much closer to the style of incensing at Benediction. As the minister moves around the coffin (without hurrying since there is a song going on), he/she stops on each side, faces the coffin, and incenses with three, full, arm-length swings. Thus the body is clearly being venerated as a temple of the Holy Spirit, and the rising smoke says farewell. The narrow aisles of some churches can make such full gestures more difficult, but *some* vigorous action is crucial here.

Note that this sign or gesture of farewell may be done in silence or may be done during the song.

COMMUNAL SONG

The fourth element, the song of farewell, is given the same prominence as in the 1969 service.

> The song of farewell, which should affirm hope and trust in the paschal mystery, is the climax of the rite of final commendation. It should be sung to a melody simple enough for all to sing. It may take the form of a responsory or even a hymn. (#147)

The introduction still repeats the directive of the 1969 service that "when singing is not possible, invocations may be recited by the assembly" (#147), but no texts for such recited invocations are provided (spoken options found in the former rite do not even appear in the appendix). We are asked to get on with the business of making the final commendation as effective as possible by expressing our emotions and common faith *in song*.

This sort of communal song offers us rich opportunities and some real difficulties. Textually some of the suggested responsories are not all that useful. Of the seven listed in #403, the second and third ("I tremble before you, ashamed of the things I have done") are hardly marked by a spirit of confident farewell. The seventh option, the ancient text set in "limbo" with Christ shattering the gates of bronze, has had its refrain changed. Rather than "You brought them light to let them see your face," we have the odd request: "Deliver me, Lord, from the streets of darkness."

Musically there are some interesting settings of the prior translations still available from ICEL in the *Resource Collection* (GIA Publications, Inc., 7404 South Mason Avenue, Chicago IL 60638). Because of their varying degrees of musical difficulty, these pieces need to be used with some prudence; yet they can be a moving experience if well done with a congregation that is familiar with them.

The OCF includes as the fifth option a two-stanza, long-meter version of "I know that my Redeemer lives" that just about any American congregation could sing on sight. Available in the "Liturgy of the Hours" section of the rite are seven other metrical hymns. The last one of these, "May saints and angels lead you on" (suggested tune: Tallis' Canon), could work quite well. Moreover, there is the standard repertory of Easter hymns, some of which *might* be appropriate. Even singing four stanzas of "Amazing Grace" at this point could be right for some gatherings. There is also the whole repertory of responsorial song. The ultimate criterion must be what the assembly can sing. In ecumenical situations especially, a metrical hymn to a familiar tune can bring a group together.

Above all we should not give up on the possibility of singing. Almost any group can follow the lead of one good voice, even *a capella*. Consider such a simple rite as the Deiss' "Keep in mind" sung as a refrain between recited verses from the "Saints of God" responsory.

Be careful, though, of too much music at the end of the funeral liturgy. The sequence of communion song/song of farewell/recessional can overwhelm a congregation if it is not handled well. A meditation song after communion would almost always completely overload the service with music.

The fifth element, the prayer of commendation, has been supplemented with an alternative form that previously appeared only in the appendix. Both of them are quite general.

Last, there is now a ministerial invitation to the recessional: "In peace let us take our brother/sister to his/her place of rest." This is a welcome smoothing-out of what had often been an awkward moment with no one quite sure what to do. Yet this invitation to escort the body of the deceased to his/her place of rest seems to be too restricted. A majority of the congregation will probably not be going to the cemetery. Consequently, a less specific invitation would be more fitting. "Let us go forth in peace!" Alleluia might be added. This could be spoken or sung and would invite the response: "Thanks be to God."

That is what we must strive to do in this rite. In spite of loss and rage and fear, we must say farewell in peace to our departed. And if we can say farewell in Christ, then the alleluias will not stick in our throats. They will be the song of those who are making that same journey to the new Jerusalem where God will be our light and the Lamb our glory.

CHAPTER 7

THE RITE OF COMMITTAL

God lives in the events of our daily lives. Upon this awareness the Jewish and Christian traditions are founded.

Israel pondered the workings of nature and discovered the creator, pondered their history and discovered the liberator. Even in catastrophe and exile and concentration camps, Israel has found a faithful God.

We Christians look at a baby in a manger and see a self-emptied God. We look at an instrument of torture and speak of the glorious cross. We look at a body wrapped hurriedly and laid in a borrowed tomb—and talk of the seed lying in the ground. As Paul says, we either are crazy or are dealing with reality in some way beyond the superficial.

Yet we live in a culture obsessed with the superficial. Advertising constantly tells us that image *is* reality. Buy this, wear that, travel in this, own that—and everybody will be impressed and we will be happy. After an evening's worth of television, you will know that both commercials and shows are still dominated by white, middle-class consumer stereotypes of whom few are over 40. There may *be* dying aplenty, but there's really no death.

We do not touch corpses; we leave that to the mortician. We do not even see corpses but rather cosmetic camouflage. We do not see genuine coffins but elaborate portable boudoirs with satin sheets and innerspring mattresses. And often we see nothing at all since we are attending a "memorial service" held for the convenience of the mourners.

The God who meets us in our scripture calls us to corpses and to things like gaping holes in the ground and the hollow thump of a spadeful of dirt hitting the lid of the box. He calls us to pain and separation and loneliness because they are part of reality, a necessary part. We will find a new part of ourselves in them. And we will find God.

THE GRAVE: INTEGRAL TO THE RITE

The concluding rite in the funeral ensemble of rites, the committal, presents its own peculiar challenges. On the one hand, it is obvious that the funeral journey needs a conclusion. The outward journey ends with some final disposition of the body; the inward journey should achieve a symbolic enactment of the new relationship between the deceased and those left behind:

> The rite marks the separation in this life of the mourners from the deceased. . . . The committal can help the mourners to face the end of one relationship with the deceased and to begin a new one based on prayerful remembrance, gratitude, and the hope of resurrection and reunion. (Order of Christian Funerals, #213)

Yet the final and irrevocable character of the committal causes great difficulty. The moment's reality cannot be denied; the anguish of separation can be intense. And so we Americans have been devising ways to run from the reality. We leave the body at a cemetery chapel to be interred later. If we get to the graveside, not only has the hole been covered up, but frequently even the dirt has been removed from view or at least covered with plastic grass. Neither gravediggers nor equipment can be seen. Rarely do we see the coffin lowered into the ground or placed into the mausoleum.

The experience of those in bereavement work is that such a postponement of separation is neither emotionally healthy nor pastorally sound. The emotions are there already: what better place or time to express them than amid the support of family and friends and with the prayer of the church? (Cf. #206 and #213.)

The major difference in the new rite is its encouragement of the *act* of committal; that "act" is the final disposition of the remains. The 1969 rite had presumed the interment as part of or the immediate sequel to the words of the service. Because that has seldom happened, the OCF now spells out that the optimum practice is *carrying out the final disposition of the body as an integral part of the rite*. The rubric is clear: "The act of committal takes place after the words of committal or at the conclusion of the rite." (#209) By "act of committal" is meant just that: putting the body into the grave or the place of interment. The purpose is also clear: "The act of committal is a stark and powerful expression of this separation . . . carried out in the midst of the community of faith." (#213) And: "Through this act the community of faith proclaims that the grave or place of interment, once a sign of futility and despair, has been transformed by means of Christ's own death and resurrection into a sign of hope and promise." (#209)

If we would carry out the rite, we would find that Christians, doing fully the rites they know well, are rehearsing the kingdom they proclaim.

CEMETERIES AND THE RITE OF COMMITTAL

To be realistic, though, many things lie in the way of achieving this optimum situation.

Many cemeteries do not encourage such a practice. In some places, costly chapels have been built to house "graveside" services; the cemetery expenses are less if interments can then be scheduled to use the time of employees most efficiently. Other expenses such as tents, chairs, walkways and liability insurance can also be minimized with a service in the chapel. It is easy to understand why some cemeteries treat an actual committal as a virtual impossibility. At best, the committal will add to the family's expenses.

There are some families for whom that extra expense is significant—and that needs to be respected. Sometimes, though, the suggestion should be made that the resources available be arranged with a different set of priorities. Money saved through a less expensive coffin could be used for the graveside committal. Bereavement ministers should not ordinarily become involved in helping the family price coffins, but part of the catechesis of parish preaching and education should deal with such questions of priority and stewardship.

There are also other sound reasons for not having the full rite: inclement weather, the advanced age of the chief mourners, some other physical handicap. The new rite provides many textual options for many circumstances. After such a chapel committal, the family and other mourners should be encouraged to visit the actual grave or mausoleum as soon as possible. Such a visit can be very helpful in the process of grief, especially if some of the prayers, readings and psalms found in the OCF are used then. Cemetery personnel are usually most helpful at facilitating such visits.

Yet even as necessary adjustments are made, we should keep the optimum as the criterion for our decisions. Those involved in bereavement work should frequently ask themselves: How well do we support the mourners in this final step of the journey by the proclamation of faith?

Invitation
Scripture Verse
Prayer over the Place of Committal
Committal
Intercessions
The Lord's Prayer
Concluding Prayer
Prayer over the People

After a newly-composed invitation and a scripture verse, the first major element in the rite is the blessing of the final resting place. To the four prayers already available (three of these are found at #405) have been added two new ones (#218-B and #218-C). The first of these is intended for situations when the place of committal has already been blessed. Though this answers a real need that mourners have to hear the words of faith proclaimed over an empty grave or tomb, the prayer itself may be too wordy. Approximately twice as long as any other option, it is structured as three invocations with a communal refrain: "Blessed is the Lord, our God!" The invocations are very general. These are followed by a prayer:

As we make ready our brother's/sister's resting-place,
look also with favor on those who mourn
and comfort them in their loss. (#218-B)

The second new composition is intended for situations in which the final disposition of the body will take place later, as in cases of cremation or when interment must be delayed. Again, this prayer meets a real need and speaks succinctly, yet appropriately to the mourners' feelings:

As we take leave of our brother/sister
and entrust his/her body to the care of others,
give our hearts peace in the firm hope
that one day N. will live
in the mansion you have prepared for him/her in heaven. (#218-C)

The biblical reading and responsorial psalm which formerly occurred next in the service have been reduced in most instances to a single scripture verse before the prayer of blessing. When a period of time, even overnight, has elapsed since the funeral liturgy or when the committal is celebrated by a different community, the rite should be filled out with one or more readings, a psalm, a brief homily, or even song (#211). Pastoral sensitivity to concrete circumstances is essential in determining if and how the service should be expanded. What works in a mortuary chapel might not on a rainy hillside. What works with fifty mourners might not with five.

Next are the words of committal. The formula from the 1969 rite has been retranslated (#219-A). It is followed (#219-B) by an alternative text taken verbatim from the 1979 Episcopalian *Book of Common Prayer.* This choice seems to be not only ecumenically gracious but also an acknowledgment of two other realities. First, many gatherings at funerals in this country are denominationally mixed. Second, Roman Catholics now have available in this option those words of committal which are probably most imbedded in the English-speaking tradition: "Earth to earth, ashes to ashes, dust to dust . . . in sure and certain hope of the resurrection to eternal life."

Two other texts for the words of committal are found at #406. One of these is for ashes, the other for burial at sea.

In some cases, the words of committal may be made more powerful if the presider asks that all repeat a few of them after they are spoken. The presider must then speak loudly and clearly, breaking the text into repeatable phrases. In some circumstances, all might extend their hands toward the coffin during the words of committal.

After the words of committal, the rubrics say that the committal is to take place, or it may come at the conclusion of the service (#219).

Immediately after the words (and action) of committal come the intercessions. There are now three options. The first is familiar from the old rite; the second is from the old rite as well, only now it appears in the body of the text rather than in the appendix (#220). The other option is found at #407.

The suggestion is made (#220) that these intercessions be adapted to circumstances or even that new ones be composed. Once again our energies need not all be focused on the funeral liturgy in the church; the other services have their own power if done with prior preparation. One of the family or a friend of the deceased could be the assisting minister who speaks the petitions.

The intercessions, as in the 1969 rite, lead into the Lord's Prayer and a concluding collect chosen from five prayers basically identical with those in the former rite. Whatever one's opinion about the gesture of joining hands at eucharist during the Lord's Prayer, nonverbal gestures of support and sharing are very much needed at this final leave-taking.

The final element is a "Prayer over the People" (#223). After the invitation, there is a time of silence, then a blessing in the form of a collect. Finally there is inserted a final intercession for the deceased in the traditional series of verses and responses: "Eternal rest . . ." etc. Then follows another blessing using a trinitarian formula, and a simple dismissal.

Though the words and images in this section are quite strong, the duplication of blessings and the mixing of different types of prayers seem ineffective.

A certain flow is created by using the word "peace" as a verbal link between different prayers, but that will not save this portion of the service from being experienced as jumbled. Simplification would not be difficult.

Well-chosen music at the end is "desirable" (#214) and often very effective. Some final gestures are permitted (#223). Soil, and flowers as is customary in some ethnic traditions, may be placed on the coffin (#210). The concluding blessing and dismissal speak of God's peace, and in most places it is customary for everyone to exchange a final word of comfort and peace with the chief mourners. Care should be taken in both the policy toward and practice of parish funerals that tributes paid by military or other societies neither detract from nor become confused with the rites of the church.

This service of committal does not seem to be as clear and powerful as the other rites in the OCF. It lacks the sense of being caught up in a rhythm of gesture, word and prayer that can lead us through something as basic and as potentially shattering as the burial of one we knew and loved. There is a danger: its many words, especially ministerial words, could just go on and on. Those who will lead this rite will do well to find ways (including those suggested in OCF) for the rite to be more involving for all who participate in it.

COMMITTAL WITH FINAL COMMENDATION

One possible adaptation clearly provided for involves combining the final commendation and the committal:

> [This] form is used when the final commendation does not take place during the funeral liturgy or when no funeral liturgy precedes the committal rite. (#205)

The former rite had given further advice about when such a combination might be desirable. There the combined rite was suggested when almost the whole congregation at the funeral liturgy would be present at the committal. In those places where the graveyard is next to the church or where custom expects everyone to join the cortege, the rite seems an effective adaptation.

Moreover, the second situation described above should probably be interpreted broadly. In our mobile America, it is not uncommon for the bulk of the funeral rites to be celebrated in one place with interment in another part of the country. The community that gathers for the committal would probably benefit from the fuller rite, perhaps even with additional scripture.

The structure of the combined rites shows how the usual texts of the two services are simply interlocked:

Committal	Committal with Final Commendation
Invitation	Invitation
Scripture Verse	Scripture Verse
Prayer over the Place of Committal	Prayer over the Place of Committal
Committal [with text]	Invitation to Prayer
Intercessions	Silence
The Lord's Prayer	Signs of Farewell (Holy Water, Incense)
Concluding Prayer	
Prayer over the People	Song of Farewell
	Prayer of Commendation
	Committal [with text]
	Prayer over the People

The most obvious difference is the omission of the formula of committal since the prayer of commendation is similar both in purpose and in language. Retaining the committal formula instead would be logical *if* done as a communal recitation. There are enough ministerial words; the assembled people need an opportunity to express themselves aloud even in the combined rite.

A potential problem with the combined rite could be the difficulty of carrying out the final commendation in a gracious and thorough manner. The song of farewell and the gestures of farewell must be strong parts of this rite.

REPETITION OF THE RITE

A very crucial point about the rite of committal is that it may and sometimes should be repeated (#212). First, if the weather or some other circumstances delay burial, the rite of committal is celebrated in the cemetery chapel. Later it may be repeated by the graveside at the actual interment.

Second, if the body is to be cremated, the rite should be celebrated at the end of the funeral liturgy in the crematory or mortuary chapel. Later it may be repeated when the ashes are buried or entombed.

Third, if the body has been donated to science, there would be no committal at a liturgy in memory of the deceased (with no body present). However, the rite of committal should be celebrated when interment of the body or ashes takes place (after the medical school has returned the body).

Two important points should also be noted about donations to science. First, the remains should ultimately be returned to the mourners for final disposition. Second, medical schools now do not object to preliminary embalming. In other words, donation to science does not necessarily prevent having the full ensemble of funeral rites. All the rites up to and including the final commendation could take place with the body present.

Those called upon to preside at a committal will find the introduction helpful. There are a number of suggestions in OCF #211 and #212 on how to adapt each committal to the specific circumstances.

CHAPTER 8

MUSIC

MUSIC IN THE PRELIMINARY RITES

"Music becomes particularly important in the new burial rites. Without it the themes of hope and resurrection are very difficult to express." (*Music in Catholic Worship*, #83)

The participants in the Vigil (wake) or other preliminary rites can be enabled to sing. All that is needed is a cantor capable of leading *a capella* singing. The flow of the rites is simple, requiring a straightforward approach to music ministry. The intimacy of a wake makes possible great intimacy in sung prayer. So it is surprising that so few parishes include music during the Vigil. Perhaps a share in this ministry should be part of every cantor's training. It certainly is a dimension of parish music which needs careful attention.

But what should be sung? Two elements have high priority:

1. The Vigil (cf. *Order of Christian Funerals*, #68)
     opening song
     responsorial psalm
   The first functions to gather a diverse group of mourners and acquaintances together as a single community ready to listen to the word of God and to pray.

Other options:
     the litany
     the Lord's Prayer
     a closing song

The repetition of a sung refrain that everyone knows is a simple but very effective way to enhance the litany. If there is someone to lead, the petitions could be sung to one of the melodies composed for the general intercessions at Mass.

Even if nothing else is sung, the Lord's Prayer can be done successfully *a capella*. The setting most familiar is the simple chant from the sacramentary.

2. The Related Rites

The psalms (#115 and #127) may be sung whenever they occur. If no one present can sing the stanzas, a refrain could be sung by all between the spoken verses. Such a use of short refrains, such as those from Taizé, adds music to these rites without the need for any printed handout. The minister simply needs to keep in mind the repertory familiar to parishioners from the Sunday liturgy.

THE FUNERAL LITURGY

As in any eucharist, sung worship is the preferred form of celebration. Communal singing is made easier and more effective by the support of trained instrumentalists and the leadership of a cantor (#153). The latter also functions as a leader of song and should be in a prominent position in full view of the assembly, not behind an organ or in a choir loft.

Those responsible for the liturgy must work from an awareness of musical priorities. Those priorities are briefly outlined in #157. The following guidelines describe a progressive enhancement of the music in the liturgy of the funeral

1. Musical core:
   Responsorial psalm
   Gospel acclamation
   Holy, holy, holy
   Memorial acclamation
   Great Amen
   Song of farewell

Five of these essential elements are known from the Sunday liturgy and of these, only the psalm might differ in text and music from the familiar Sunday melodies. As discussed in chapter 6, the song of farewell is a central element in the whole unfolding of the rites. It allows for various approaches. Thus the parish that uses strong, familiar acclamations each Sunday need only settle on a very few psalm refrains and two or three options for the song of farewell. If some version of the universally appropriate *In Paradisum* ("May the angels lead you into paradise . . .") is chosen for this song, it can be sung at all funerals and on All Souls Day, and gradually become a beloved part of the parish's repertory. Funeral psalms can also be learned on Sundays, using them within the liturgy each November. Thus the basic core of music for the funeral Mass will be already part of the parish's repertory.

2. Music enrichment:
   Processional song
   Lord's Prayer
   Lamb of God
   Communion song

If the Lord's Prayer and the Lamb of God are sung on Sundays, it may be possible to sing them during funerals. In fact, not singing the regular Sunday repertory may give the impression to parishioners that this funeral is somehow unimportant. Processional singing during the entrance and during communion may be problematic. It's not easy to read the words of songs while walking. Responsorial-style music may facilitate singing at these times. Since emotions are high during the entrance procession, perhaps instrumental music or one of the lovely Taizé ostinati would be better than a metrical hymn. After everyone is in place, with hymnals or worship programs in hand, it may be easier to sing a hymn or song.

Worship programs created especially for funerals make it possible to avoid announcements of page numbers. Programs help a congregation, many of whom are not familiar with liturgy, understand the flow of the rites. Do not include the text of prayers or readings. Programs are not for reading along. Especially in the entrance procession, the liturgical season can guide the choice of music. Read over the verses of "O Come, O Come, Emmanuel" and "Hark, the Herald Angels Sing." They would make splendid funeral songs during Advent and Christmastime, respectively.

3. Further music enrichment:
   Response to the General Intercessions
   Recessional Hymn

Again, the response to the intercessions is a simple and repetitious refrain known from the Sunday liturgy.

The recessional is presented by the OCF in #149 as particularly important because it occurs during the beginning of the last phase of the funeral journey. Yet there is a practical difficulty with its successful performance: the mourners are leaving church while it is being sung. Something very familiar or else responsorial in character seems to have the best chance of success.

For a funeral liturgy outside of Mass, the same three progressive models may be used, omitting those elements proper to the eucharistic prayer. The communion song might be included if there is to be communion from the reserved sacrament.

MUSIC AT THE COMMITTAL

The singing of well-chosen music at the rite of committal can help the mourners as they face the reality of the separation. (#214)

Many cemetery or crematory chapels have an organ to support singing. For outdoor services, portable instruments such as the flute and guitar can be used. The most crucial component, though, is one person with a good, strong voice.

Since the committal is the last stage of the journey, the OCF proposes that the procession from the funeral liturgy to the place of final disposition may be accompanied by appropriate psalms or songs (#176). If some time has elapsed since the funeral liturgy, an opening song could gather people back together in a spirit of prayer.

If the committal is to be combined with the commendation, the psalm chosen could be sung and the song of farewell should certainly be sung. The Lord's Prayer could also be sung by all.

Even the singing of a simple refrain known from the Sunday eucharist can be appropriate here. The Lamb of God would be a fitting song as would the litany of the saints.

SPECIAL REQUESTS AND REGULAR REPERTORY

People want funerals to be warm, graceful, personal and inspiring. They want a taste of heaven, of the overwhelming peace of the risen Christ, of the great hope to which we are called. Special requests for particular songs from families are often their attempt to make the funeral Mass warm and personal. But these requests—such as the Shubert "Ave," the Franck "Panis," or even "Danny Boy"—can become something of an embarrassment rather than the inspiration they were intended to be.

Special requests are frequently alien to the Mass, and rob the liturgy of its power and integrity. These intrusions in the Mass mean that we don't treat everyone equally. Certainly there is nothing inherently wrong with Shubert or Franck. They may have been sung on the deceased's wedding day. And they do have a place in the funeral rites, but that place is the vigil where, surrounded with stories of the dead and prayer, they can speak on their own.

The music at our funerals needs to be drawn from the regular music of Sunday Mass. Music drawn from the parish's singing during Eastertime and November would make fine choices. This stable repertory coupled with the presence of a cantor or choir to lead and carry a burden of the singing would enable all our funerals to be warm and graceful.

CHAPTER 9

FUNERALS OF CHILDREN

When a child has died, so many of our usual comments about death are meaningless. We cannot talk about the natural rhythm of a lifetime because that rhythm has been broken. We cannot take consolation in what the deceased had accomplished because everything had been hope and dream and not fulfillment. We cannot look at the person's children and grandchildren. We cannot even take refuge in memories since they are so few. Especially when a child has died after long illness or suffering, we fall silent, for what can we say about such pain? We are left with no explanations, no answers, no solutions. We are left with the fact of death and the mystery of God's love.

It is crucial to begin our examination of the funeral rites for children by taking a close look at the introduction to that section (*Order of Christian Funerals*, #234–242).

First, grieving for a child is communal. Here, as in the General Introduction (cf. #9–13), ministry to the bereaved is not the private task of a designated individual; rather, everyone is invited to share in the task of mutual consolation. "In its pastoral ministry to the bereaved, the Christian community is challenged in a particular way. . . . The community seeks to offer support and consolation during and after the time of the funeral rites." (#238)

Yet in answering that invitation not everyone has the same talents. "The minister should invite members of the community to use their individual gifts in this ministry of consolation." (#240)

Those who lost children of their own are to be especially encouraged to support the bereaved in their struggle to accept the death of a child (#240).

Second, the introduction makes clear that the community, in fulfilling its ministry, offers and proclaims faith, not solutions. "Christ still sorrows with those who sorrow and longs with them for the fulfillment of the Father's plan in a new creation where tears and death will have no place." (#239)

Third, a deep sensitivity for individual styles of grief is encouraged. "The bewilderment and pain that death causes can be overwhelming in this situation, especially for the parents and brothers and sisters of the deceased child." (#238) The community is invited simply to walk with the bereaved at their pace and support them whenever possible.

The texts of the rites for children consistently reinforce the outlook of the introduction. No answers are proposed, no guilt is placed on anyone. Instead there are repeated references to the image of God as "holding" the deceased child:

> Comfort us with the knowledge that N. is already at peace in your loving arms. (#282-B)

> For N., child of God . . . that he/she be held securely in God's loving embrace now and for all eternity. (#285)

> Loving God, you now hold this little one N. in your arms and caress him/her in your kindness. (#325-A)

How could that image help the mourners live through the mystery of a child's death? A nurse in the intensive care unit of a hospital for children explains this in a story. She tries to help parents take care of themselves during a crisis for their child. Numb with exhaustion, they still cannot leave their child's side. She knows there is only one sentence she can speak to reassure the parents: she tells them simply that she will hold the child if the child begins to cry. Parents need not believe that the nurse will end the child's pain, only that she will be there to share in it. Then they can rest for a while.

These words we share with the bereaved help them to realize what we believe: that their child is now "in God's arms." Then they can begin to rest a bit, to let go and move further into the mystery. They can discover that they too are being held in God's arms.

Outline of the Rites: Vigil for a Deceased Child

Introductory Rites

Greeting
Sprinkling with Holy Water or Brief Address
[Placing of the Pall]

Entrance Procession
[Placing of Christian Symbols]
Invitation to Prayer
Opening Prayer

Liturgy of the Word

First Reading
Responsorial Psalm
Gospel
Homily

Prayer of Intercession

Litany
The Lord's Prayer
Concluding Prayer

Concluding Rite
Blessing

Funeral Mass

Introductory Rites
Greeting
Sprinkling with Holy Water or Brief Address
[Placing of the Pall]
Entrance Procession
[Placing of Christian Symbols]
Opening Prayer

Liturgy of the Word

Readings
Homily
General Intercessions

Liturgy of the Eucharist

Final Commendation

Invitation to Prayer
Silence
[Signs of Farewell]
Song of Farewell
Prayer of Commendation

Procession to the Place of Committal

Rite of Committal
Invitation
Scripture Verse
Prayer over the Place of Committal
Committal
Intercessions
The Lord's Prayer
Concluding Prayer
Prayer over the People

Rite of Final Commendation for an Infant
Brief Address
Scripture Verse
Blessing of the Body
The Lord's Prayer
Prayer of Commendation
Blessing

What is immediately evident is the improvement over the 1969 book. There the options for children were fewer, less adaptable, scattered throughout the text. Now the three major rites, vigil, funeral liturgy and committal, flow coherently and are grouped together as a separate section, "Funeral Rites for Children." The outlines above give a good idea of how helpful the OCF is. Much of what follows here will address what is still lacking or incomplete in these rites.

We have the unfortunate omission from these rites for children of what are called the "Related Rites" in the adult section. These are the "Prayers after Death," "Gathering in the Presence of the Body" and "Transfer of the Body to the Church or the Place of Committal." These rites as they are presented for adults should, of course, be adapted by the minister to the circumstances (#234), but we are given little help for that adaptation. For example, the blessing of the deceased which plays a strong role in the "Related Rites" should have a different introduction in the funeral of a child:

Jesus said: "Let the children come to me. Do not keep them from me. The kingdom of God belongs to such as these." (#263)

Yet the minister can find this text only in the vigil service of the section for children.

One welcome addition is the new "Rite of Final Commendation for an Infant," intended "in the case of a stillborn or a newborn infant who dies shortly after birth" (#318). It is a form of final commendation meant for the hospital or place of committal. As such, its words and imagery are beautiful:

Trusting in Jesus, the loving Redeemer . . . we now commend this infant N. to that same embrace of love. (#339)

One difficulty in this particular rite comes in the "Blessing of the Body" (#339). Here a song of farewell might have been one option. Instead, the OCF substitutes a ministerial blessing of the body in which everyone recites together the central section:

May the angels and saints lead him/her
to the place of light and peace
where one day
we will be reunited with him/her.

The words are fairly strong, but handing out cards so that everyone can recite together destroys the possibility of people touching and holding each other during the rite. It might be better done with the presiding minister simply asking everyone to recite phrase by phrase following his or her lead. If the minister or the parents could also touch the body during the blessing, the action would strongly reinforce the words.

THE FUNERAL LITURGY

In the funeral liturgy itself (the central rite, whether within or outside Mass), the reception rite for an unbaptized child seems ritually impoverished. Rather than the sprinkling with holy water and the spreading of the white pall, there is a "Brief Address" by the presiding minister before the Easter candle leads the procession into the church.

Granted, the pall is associated so strongly with baptism that its use would be inauthentic. The minister, though, could lay a hand on the coffin during the brief address as a gesture of welcome. Moreover, if the baptismal faith of the parents is the reason the church will bury their child with most of our rites (cf. #237), could we not use holy water as part of the reception? Sprinkling the family and possibly the whole community while saying appropriate words might be a strong gesture.

In the final commendation for an unbaptized child, there is again to be no sprinkling with holy water, but why the lack of incense? If we are going to celebrate the funeral liturgy, then the body of an unbaptized child deserves that gesture of reverence. (Reverence, not purification, is the significance of the incensation here. Cf. #147.) The song of farewell needs to be reinforced by action, and the rising cloud of incense speaks strongly of commendation (cf. #37).

Similarly, for both an unbaptized and a baptized child, there is a need for a truly appropriate song of farewell. The first one proposed in the text, the fourth of the responsories given in #403, is a good choice for this service because it speaks of the child's life in God to parents and family who have seen earthly life so early ended. The fifth option in #403 (a metrical version of the fourth) seems equally appropriate. Most of the other responsories are not. Clearly, additional compositions are needed, especially those that the children present can join in singing. The major difference in selecting a song of farewell for a child is making certain that the images have a certain tenderness to them.

THE RITE OF COMMITTAL

In the graveside rite of committal, the OCF itself contains a parallel adaptation to what is suggested above for the song of farewell. Here, in the rite of committal for a baptized child, the only significant difference from the rite for adults is in the actual words of committal. The standard options appear in the appendix, but in the body of the text there is found a new formula, one borrowed from the Episcopal tradition.

Into your hands, O merciful Savior, we commend N.
Acknowledge, we humbly beseech you,
a sheep of your own fold, a lamb of your own flock.
Receive him/her into the arms of your mercy,
into the blessed rest of everlasting peace,
and into the glorious company of the saints in light. (#322-A)

It is unfortunate that this text was not arranged so that everyone could recite it together, phrase by phrase, following the minister.

THE READINGS

In the midst of a generally successful adaptation and development, there is one glaring failure—the lectionary. Out of the riches of the scriptures, it seems incomprehensible to suggest so few appropriate passages. There are, for example, only two selections from the whole of the Hebrew Bible.

Nor do some of the options make sense. The cross was Jesus' path to glory—a fact which one of the texts for the presentation of a cross as part of the reception rite states rather touchingly:

The cross we have brought here today was carried by the Lord Jesus in the hour of his suffering. We place it now on [near] this coffin as a sign of our hope for N. (#400)

64

Yet to suggest the crucifixion (two of the three options for an unbaptized child) as the gospel of the funeral liturgy is insensitive. The parents and family will not find the graphic details of the narrative to be good news. They need instead to be reassured that they as well as their child are held in God's hands. As the first gospel option (the one *invariably* chosen for the service) so simply says: "Come to me all you who labor and are over-burdened, and I will give you rest." (Matthew 11:28) Surely other appropriate texts can be added to this funeral lectionary.

THE PRESENCE OF CHILDREN

One of the most important aspects of the funeral of a child is that it usually involves other children. Brothers and sisters, cousins, neighborhood friends, classmates—all can be caught in the same grief which adults are experiencing and with fewer skills for dealing with such emotion. The introduction to this section in the OCF refers to this fact more than once:

> Special consideration should be given to any sisters, brothers, friends or classmates of the deceased child who may be present at the funeral rites. . . . The minister may wish to offer brief remarks for the children's benefit at suitable points during the celebration. (#242)

Children should be involved in preparing and celebrating the funeral of someone they loved. The *Directory for Masses with Children* is referred to in #242 of the OCF as a guide in adaptation.

The *Directory* groups its services under two headings: those celebrated by adults with some children and those celebrated by children with some adults. It avoids any rigid categorization into what is or is not "children's liturgy." Instead, it even suggests ways in which portions even of Sunday Mass could be adapted.

> Some account should be taken of their presence: for example, by speaking to them directly in the introductory comments . . . and at some point in the homily. (*Directory*, #17)

The *Directory* recognizes that some services will involve mostly children, but is insistent that adults should not feel excluded (cf. *Directory*, #24). Moreover, the goal of "children's liturgy" is not to isolate them but to initiate them gradually into the adult prayer life of the church. It would be unfortunate if overzealous adaptations for children during the rites would prevent adults from taking their own proper roles.

Adaptation for children does not mean that cute can replace competent. Tommy may be the spitting image of his grandfather, but he should not be a server unless he knows when to bring out the holy water and how to carry the Easter candle. Susie may have been the deceased's closest friend, but if she can't read aloud with comprehension and feeling, she should not be proclaiming the scriptures. We should be prepared to take the time and effort to teach children, initiating them into their place within worship. Patience, consideration and flexibility are needed in preparing competent ministers of worship, regardless of age.

WHAT IS SUGGESTED FOR CHILDREN?

First, children can be involved in preparing the more intimate surroundings of the wake. There the visual elements which the *Directory* encourages and which were discussed above in chapter 3 could have a very significant role to play. Moreover, the classmates and friends of a deceased child could arrange one of the related rites or a similar service under the guidance of teachers and others. Such celebrations play a major role in children's preparation for the adult liturgical life of the church (*Directory*, #13–14).

Second, they may exercise some of the liturgical roles (acolytes, musicians, etc.) *if* they have the "requisite ability" (#242). They enjoy and do best at the nonverbal roles. As the *Directory* points out, children particularly enjoy processions (*Directory*, #34); being part of the gospel procession or helping in a real presentation of the gifts are tasks at which they could succeed—if they are rehearsed in advance.

However, it is most important that no child ever be pressured into a role which he or she really does not want. Respect for individual styles of grief must apply to children as well as adults.

Perhaps the most important suggestion in the *Directory* is the importance of sung participation in the eucharistic prayer. Much depends on the manner in which the priest proclaims this prayer and on the way the children take part by listening and making their acclamations. (*Directory*, #52)

> If possible, the acclamations should be sung by the children rather than recited, especially the acclamations that form part of the eucharistic prayer. (*Directory*, #30)

In the Eucharistic Prayers for Masses with Children, frequent, repetitious acclamations create a sense of communal prayer. One should not spring unfamiliar music on a congregation, but *some* sung acclamations should be familiar to the gathering.

Eucharistic Prayer III for Masses with Children has special texts for use during Eastertime. In accessible scriptural words it proclaims the mystery both of our crucified and risen Lord and of our share in his glory. This prayer, with its Eastertime texts, works well with a congregation of adults and children; it would be equally successful at the funeral of a child or one attended by many children. This text is found in Appendix VI of the 1985 editions of the sacramentary. There are two cautions. First, the special Eastertime changes are printed at the bottom of the page. Either the presider must be well rehearsed in the text or he must be provided with the Eastertime text in a typed-out version. Second, there is no special memento for the deceased. The presider might compose a brief intercession of his own or adapt one (from Eucharistic Prayer II for Masses with Children, for example).

In the funeral of a child, the community is challenged to use a diversity of gifts to support those members who are in pain and grief. We are all drawn into the mystery of God's reign which is really among us—but not yet, not fully. Here we discover how much faith and hope and love are intertwined: "And this hope is not deceptive, because the love of God has been poured into our hearts by the Holy Spirit which has been given us." (Romans 5:5)

APPENDIX

A. CREMATION

For almost 20 years cremation has been a canonical option for Roman Catholics:

> Funeral rites are to be granted to those who have chosen cremation, unless there is evidence that their choice was dictated by anti-Christian motives. (1969 *Ordo Exsequiarum*, #15)

Indeed, except for those aware of disputes in previous centuries with Masons and Deists about personal immortality, such "anti-Christian motives" seem a little hard to imagine. What does motivate an individual or a family, though, to choose cremation? From my experience, the predominant reasons are two: personal preference and financial considerations.

The first choice, a person's own preference, should be respected— even if we disagree with the reasoning behind the decision. A dear friend who died three years ago was cremated by her own choice. As she had explained several times, the process of physical decay was repugnant to her; she preferred a way which seemed to her neat and clean by comparison. Though she loved nature and the God of nature, the argument that burial was somehow less violent and more natural held no weight with her. In current church law she had every right to her choice.

What of the family in such a case? In this instance, the family—in the judgment of the parish's bereavement ministry—was using cremation as an escape from the process of grieving. Only after some urging did they agree not only to a memorial Mass but to a reception afterwards. Halfway through the service the stoic composure that they had maintained began to break. The reception turned into a great party in which, through tears and laughter, the family discovered how much their wife and mother had meant to all of us—and so really began the process of saying farewell.

For far too many people in the death-denying culture of America, cremation is the easy way out. This is corroborated by funeral directors. As one said, she has hundreds of unclaimed urns in storage awaiting final disposition.

The second motive for choosing cremation, finances, should be a major question not only for those of limited means but also for any Christian concerned about responsible stewardship. Cremation immediately following death eliminates the cost of embalming, casket, use of the funeral home for a wake, transportation to several places by hearse, a large cemetery plot, a concrete liner, and the labor of opening and closing the grave. Clearly we are talking here about a significant financial consideration.

Yet the monetary saving is relative. The body must still be transported to the crematory. By law it must be burned *inside* a container. The oven must run for a number of hours. Some sort of metal container or urn is needed to hold the cremated remains. And final disposition of the container with its remains must be made either by burial or in some form of columbarium. Cheaper is still not cheap.

Nor should ecological concerns be ignored. One need only drive out the Long Island Expressway to see what a consumer of land an urban cemetery can become. Perhaps even earth burial should not give the deceased permanent title to the property. There are many ethnic traditions (some of them Catholic and as close to us as New Orleans) where the remains are reverently exhumed after a year or so when the process of decomposition has done its work and then reinterred in a vault or much smaller plot. Yet, though we Americans might appreciate the good sense of such a practice, our culturally ingrained denial of death would likely never let us consider being personally involved in exhumation.

The discussion is just beginning. One might read Robert Hovda's two excellent articles on this and related questions in his column, "The Amen Corner," in the March and May 1985 issues of *Worship.* How can American Catholics make the changes responsible stewardship might require?

Cremation in the Revised Rite

Whatever the future holds, in the funeral rites contained in the *Order of Christian Funerals* (OCF) it is presumed that *immediate* cremation will not occur. Instead cremation is understood to take place *after* the various rites (except committal). Since that is not the usual procedure, Roman Catholic families and funeral directors need to be informed of the fact as soon as possible to avoid misunderstandings.

The procedure the OCF envisions is this: a wake, one or more of the related rites, the full funeral liturgy, and committal at the crematory. Nothing would vary from a service with burial except for the location of the committal. Perhaps, though, it should be called the first committal, for the committal may be repeated when the cremated remains are to be buried or entombed (*Order of Christian Funerals*, #212).

There is a need to use the options outlined in the OCF (and in chapter 7 of this book) to make each committal as effective as possible. The need for gestures and physical contact and support is as great at cremation or final disposition of the ashes as at earth burial.

Cremation before the Rites

It seems clear that not everyone will follow the procedure preferred by OCF. From ignorance or strong preference, some will choose immediate cremation for the deceased. What can the church and her ministers do to avoid alienating these people? Pastorally, what can we find in the OCF for this situation?

First, before the body leaves the hospital or wherever death occurred, the service for "Gathering in the Presence of the Body" should be held for the family and other mourners. There is still the deep need for them to reverence the corpse so that the reality of death and of faith may be evoked. The rite with its sprinkling of holy water and marking with the sign of the cross meets that need—especially if some of the adaptations suggested in chapter 4 are used. With this service a sense of the funeral journey's beginning could be experienced.

Moreover, the ending of the journey can be experienced. At the crematory, the "Rite of Committal with Final Commendation" (chapters 6 and 11 in OCF) could be celebrated since there was no commendation in church:

> The [Rite of Committal with Final Commendation] is used when the final commendation does not take place during the funeral liturgy or when no funeral liturgy precedes the committal rite. (#205)

The same service could be held *after* the cremation at the time of final disposition of the cremated remains (#212). With song and holy water and incense the ashes can be reverenced and then entombed or interred.

Other major Christian churches in this country and in Europe have allowed the cremated remains rather than the body to be the focus of the rites. Moreover, in an indult dated March 11, 1985, the Congregation for Divine Worship granted the Canadian bishops permission to allow the full ensemble of rites—including the eucharist—in the presence of the ashes of the deceased. Though the indult does not encourage immediate cremation, it does permit what seems a needed option. Only seven possible changes were needed in the French ritual to make the words appropriate for the new situation. (Cf. the Canadian *Bulletin national de liturgie*, septembre–octobre 1985, pp. 156–158.)

Cremation should not mean a loss of ritual. The full use of rites helps mourners begin the process of grieving, and offers them an integrated funeral journey. As one mourner remarked, it seems wrong to leave the ashes in the car during the funeral. If religious rites are celebrated at the columbarium, then why not in the church building?

There may be difficulties in giving honor to ashes with the white pall and water. A small cloth draping an urn may not evoke the white garments of baptism. But certainly the paschal candle, generous use of both water and incense, and a dignified but tender treatment of an urn would be ways to reverence the ashes of our dead. The OCF's option for cremation following the funeral rites is altogether understandable, but the next years will tell whether other options may be needed.

B. FUNERAL CHOIRS

Even in parishes with splendid music on Sundays, music can be poor at funerals. Of course, a good cantor can provide the necessary musical leadership. However, many communities are finding the establishment of a funeral choir an antidote to poor or haphazard music ministry at parish funerals.

Funeral choirs are a way to assure that all parishioners are buried with dignity and beauty, surrounded by other members of the parish as well as family and friends. Funerals, of course, are for the living, and a funeral choir expresses the commitment of parishioners to each other and to all who gather to celebrate the funeral liturgy.

Who Would Join?

At first it might be difficult to imagine who would commit to such a choir. After all, most folks are not available during the day. But every parish has homemakers who might be able to come at this time, especially if child care services are made available during funerals. Also, retired people can be encouraged to join. A funeral choir can be the most important contribution senior citizens make to parish liturgy, increasing their self-esteem and sharing their talents. As one fellow said, "Heck, I'd be going to most of these funerals anyway. Why not give me this chance to help?"

How do you begin? Advertise! Use the less effective vehicles of the parish bulletin, parish announcements at Mass and direct appeals to senior citizens' groups and to other parish choirs. And use the more effective vehicle of one-to-one conversations (begging). Explain to people as vividly as possible what parish funerals can be like with the help of a funeral choir. Let people in on your vision of possibilities. Set a date for the first rehearsal, or for convenience set two dates so excuses come twice as hard.

Organize this first rehearsal tightly. Nobody wants to commit time to inefficiency. But plan for socializing, perhaps during a break. Warm up with familiar music before trying something like singing in canon. Give those in attendance an immediate sense of how satisfying choral singing can be, even with a single rehearsal.

Create reasonable expectations for attendance at funerals. Don't expect anyone to come to more than about ten funerals a month, if that. Especially if you have a large number of funerals, formulate a system so members can keep a commitment (with some flexibility) to specific days of the week (Gladys comes to Monday, Wednesday and Friday funerals . . .).

Aim for a choir of about a dozen members at any given funeral. At first, only six or so will suffice. After the first rehearsal, distribute members' names and numbers, and ask for volunteers to make the necessary phone calls before a funeral. Further rehearsals might not be needed, especially if the choir warms up and practices a half hour or so before each funeral. Recruitment will be a continuing need. Don't be discouraged, since some people will join only after they've heard an established group, and a few members will quit after discovering they really can't spare the time. Don't take things personally.

Although a funeral choir may seem potentially depressing, the outpouring of appreciation for this ministry from families of the dead, from other parishioners and from funeral directors will energize the group. Don't overlook the possibilities of employing the funeral choir at other parish liturgies from time to time. Daytime holy day liturgies and great parish feasts would benefit from their presence.

As with any parish organization, the funeral choir needs recognition during Sunday worship by both pastor and parish leaders. And they need a bit of fun, too, in the form of a picnic or party or even an excursion.

Repertory

Every parishioner deserves to be buried with dignity as an equal member of the community we call parish. The funeral choir can promise this dignity at a liturgy that is warm and graceful.

Try deciding on music for the funeral liturgy that is equally appropriate for all parish funerals. This isn't as difficult as it might seem. Psalm 23 ("The Lord is my shepherd") is a universally appropriate psalm for the liturgy of the word or for communion. *In Paradisum* ("May the angels lead you into paradise") is a fitting song for any final commendation. The choir might sing by themselves during the preparation of the gifts, varying this music with the liturgical seasons to give the choir a welcome challenge.

Repeating the same well-chosen music for all parish funerals means you will be more successful in establishing this music in people's memories. Try using this music during the month of November or during Eastertime at Sunday Mass.